Sober Play

Using Creativity for a More Joyful Recovery

Jill Kelly
with Bridget Benton

Sober Play: Using Creativity for a More Joyful Recovery

Copyright © 2013 by Jill Beverly Kelly, PhD

Excerpts from *The Creative Tao* by Pamela K. Metz reprinted with permission from Humanix Publishing, 560 Village Blvd., West Palm Beach, FL 33409.

3Cats Publishing
1932 SE Ash
Portland, OR 97214
www.jillkellyauthor.com
jill@jillkellyauthor.com

Book Design
Amy Livingstone, Sacred Art Studio
www.sacredartstudio.net

ISBN-13: 978-0615760117 (3 Cats Publishing)
ISBN-10: 0615760112

TABLE OF CONTENTS

A word about...

DEDICATION

To all of us with the courage
to climb out of the darkness of addiction
into the sunlight of the Spirit.

Sober Play
Using Creativity for a More Joyful Recovery

Creativity is a gift to every human being.
It is never used up and is always available.
No one knows where it is, or where it goes.
One only needs to trust, and there it is!

—Pamela K. Metz, *The Creative Tao*

Introduction

I got sober at 43. I had been a shy and frightened child, an angst-ridden teenager, a codependent lover, a driven student, a demanding college professor, a self-proclaimed intellectual, and a confirmed cynic. And for the 20 years before I entered a treatment center in Lynchburg, Virginia, a high-functioning drunk. But I had never seen myself as a creative or as an artist.

Today, 23 years later, creativity and artmaking are a central part of my life—and, somewhat surprisingly to me, a crucial part of my ongoing recovery from alcoholism. Many things have helped me stay sober: working the 12 Steps, thousands of meetings, working with sponsors, prayer, meditation, therapy, and perhaps most importantly, a mysterious Grace that I do not understand. But nothing has made me happier in sobriety than being actively creative.

For the last decade, as creative self-expression has become more and more of what I do and how I live, I've been struck by the parallels between successful recovery and the creative process. How the values that lead to one are just as important in the other. How when I coach writers who are stuck, I use techniques from recovery. And how when I sponsor women in recovery, I use creative process techniques to help them strengthen their sobriety.

This book is a compilation of my thinkings and learnings about the two processes: recovery and creative self-expression. I am heavily indebted to the work of Eric Maisel, Julia Cameron, Pamela K. Metz, and dozens of others including major contributor Bridget Benton*, who have taught me so much about myself and what a life can be if we open our hearts to the creative.

My hope is that the ideas and exercises in this book can open a door for you into that creative place that can strengthen sobriety and bring you some of the peace and happiness that I have found in artmaking.

*Bridget's name appears on her contributions.

Part I

Creativity as a Part of the Recovery Puzzle

When creativity is practiced, there is contentment in the world.

—Pamela K. Metz, *The Creative Tao*

1 We are each creative.

Each of us is born creative. It's a fundamental part of being human.

No one really knows what we are born with. While we are born with a tangible, physical body that can be measured and tested, nobody knows all that our minds, let alone our souls, bring when we come into this life. But among the many capacities we human beings have potential for, I believe creativity is at the center.

2 Creativity is a natural part of who we are as human beings.

Creativity is not a special skill or a talent. It is a part of being human. But like a skill or a talent, we can develop it.

Although we don't fully understand what creativity is or how it occurs in our minds or souls or bodies, none of that really matters. What we do know is what creativity lets us do. Creativity helps us respond to life and our environment in new ways. Because of our creativity, we can learn, we can change, and we can get sober.[1]

3 Addiction is a way to respond to life.

Some of us come into life with a propensity for addiction. There are many ideas about why this is so, but the *why* doesn't really matter. What does matter is whether that we act on that propensity, whether we respond to life in that way, for addiction is a response. It is a response of the body, of the mind, and perhaps even of the soul to our circumstances and to our feelings about those circumstances.

4 Addiction can be a response to dissatisfaction.

At my first beer party in college, I don't remember enjoying being tipsy or liking the taste of beer. But I didn't stop drinking until I left the party, drunk and fading in and out of blackout. My body's response was to want more. I couldn't get satisfied.

I didn't know then that I was already an addict. I don't mean from that one beer party. I mean from the decade before of eating candy and other sweets with the same gobbling abandon, the same lack of satisfaction.

---

[1] Although *sober* is a term usually used to refer to alcoholics, I use this term to designate abstinence from any form of addictive and destructive behavior.

I was 19 the first time I got drunk, but I had already had a lifetime of restlessness and anxiety. Other people seemed happy and contented, but I just couldn't find those feelings. Nothing seemed to satisfy me, and if it did, the feeling didn't last. Alcohol seemed to promise satisfaction, so I went on drinking and trying to get satisfied. The drinking didn't satisfy me either, but it made me not care that I wasn't satisfied.

5 Perhaps some of us need more satisfaction than others.

Lack of satisfaction is, for me, a critical piece of my relationship with addiction. Finding satisfaction is at the center of my relationship with creativity.

I don't know if some of us are born needing more satisfaction than other people. Or if those others just find satisfaction more easily than we do. But long before I picked up the first dozen beers, long before I crossed the line into an unstoppable craving for alcohol, I was searching for something I couldn't find.

Some believe that our use of addictive substances is a substitute for a relationship with God/Spirit/Higher Power, that we alcoholics and addicts have a "hole in the soul" that we try to fill with substances. That well may be. All I know is that I have a kind of chronic anxiety and restlessness that is often unbearable. And for five decades I used sugar, then alcohol, then sugar again in an attempt to soothe it.

6 Creative self-expression can be a support for sobriety.

The program's readings say that the missing piece is a connection to God and that service—in and out of the meetings—is the answer. I would agree that it is certainly *an* answer and a very important one. At the same time, for some of us or maybe even for all of us, service may be only part of the answer. I found another puzzle piece to a happier, more satisfied life in recovery: creative self-expression.

7 Artists vs. creatives

I am not suggesting you drop everything in your life and become a full-time artist. In fact, this book isn't about becoming an artist at all. It is about becoming a *creative*.

Artists: Those with sufficient persistence and encouragement to develop their creativity to such an extent that they can sell their work in the marketplace. A professional creative.

Creatives: Every one of us who finds the courage to follow our own path into our creative selves.

8 Many of us are reluctant to become a creative—and for good reason.

I think each of us comes into life with much more creativity than we usually recognize. But in our culture as it has evolved, we are expected to use our abilities, including our creativity, to be successful in a very narrow way. That cultural idea of success is to make a lot of money (or at least enough to support yourself and your family) and to become famous. When creative self-expression is seen through this lens, only artists, those who get paid to express themselves creatively, are seen as creatives.

In earlier times, people used creative self-expression to entertain themselves, their families, their neighbors. They gathered to sing and dance and tell stories. They didn't have to be professionals to do this. They did it for fun. They also made beautiful and useful objects to use in their daily lives or for spiritual rituals. I suspect they did it because it was natural to do so, because it was meaningful and joyful and satisfying.

Most of us are reluctant to do this. Our vast and steady exposure to professional singers, dancers, painters, sculptors, musicians has set a high standard of performance, one that makes our own efforts seem poor, perhaps laughable, perhaps impossible. ✓   *Interesting Observation*

9 *Original creativity*: The creativity we are born with[2]

Everyone has original creativity or creative potential. It includes our abilities to learn, to solve problems, to make connections, to imagine, to create new things, and to change what doesn't work in our lives, like addiction. It also includes the potential for creative self-expression.

In addition, some of us come in with certain talents. Perhaps we were born with ears already set to musical ability, like perfect pitch, thus making singing easier. Or perhaps we were born with a very wide finger span, making playing the piano easier. Maybe we were born with a certain flexibility of body, an enhanced sense of balance or gracefulness that makes dancing easier. Or we have a heightened sensitivity to color or shape or line that makes drawing and painting easier.

---

[2] The terminology and ideas of *original, formed,* and *available* are from the exciting work of Eric Maisel. See *A Natural Psychology*, 2010.

Some of us don't seem to have any discernible talent for self-expression. But we still have creativity. Everybody has original creativity; everybody has creative potential.

10 Original creativity is hard to measure.

It can be hard to discern our original creativity. We don't have conscious memories of ourselves at birth, and when we are very young, we don't have verbal language to describe our feelings and our abilities. So, on the one hand, we may have to have faith in the existence of our original creativity, in its being a natural part of who we are. On the other hand, nearly every small child will sing and dance and draw and make things at the drop of a hat. They don't need a class or an apprenticeship or their face on a magazine cover or their name on a large check to know that they are creative.

An oft-told anecdote: If you ask a classroom of first-graders who's an artist, all or nearly all hands go up. If you ask a classroom of eighth-graders the same question, one or two hands will go up.

Original creativity doesn't get lost, but it can fade from our awareness.

11 Our past influences our *formed creativity.*

Formed creativity is the relationship we have developed with our creative selves through our internal and external experiences.

If we're lucky, there was room for our creative selves in our families when we were growing up. We had access to crayons or colored pencils, paper or a coloring book, connect-the-dot workbooks to help us learn about line and shape. We had parents who expressed joy and confidence in our abilities. We had elementary school teachers who had received some training in art or in a philosophy of teaching that encouraged the development of original creativity even if they didn't call it that.

And if we were lucky, we were encouraged to draw and color, to sing and dance. To make leaf ash trays, even if nobody in the family smoked, or a paper candy cane for the Christmas tree. Most parents delight in the simple efforts of their children. They save those first drawings, those first scribbles, that first three-sentence story. My mother did. In my bathroom hang two circles of plaster painted brown, my 5-year-old hands captured in art from a kindergarten project.

Some of us weren't so lucky. There was no money for creative materials at home. Our parents were poor or didn't care or struggled too hard just to survive. Maybe we had a parent who drank and we never spent much time at home. Maybe we went to poor schools in poor neighborhoods where teachers struggled with too-large classrooms and teaching art was the last thing on their minds. Whatever the circumstance, we didn't get any exposure to art when we were young and full of original creativity.

12 What came next for most of us

Whether we had early happy experiences with creative self-expression or not, what forms our beliefs about our ability to express ourselves creatively was mostly not very encouraging. Certain kids got singled out in school for their ability to draw realistically. That became the standard. Our own efforts looked strange or paltry next to theirs and our enthusiasm faded. Or our singing voice wasn't strong enough or on-key often enough to make the chorus. Some of us tried out for the school play but we weren't good-looking enough or popular enough. Even our parents, once so eager to post every effort on the refrigerator, weren't willing to pay for music or dance lessons if we hadn't shown "talent."

During a summer school class after 8th grade, the teacher told me that my drawings were too timid, my photographs too weird to be successful. I should find something else to do, he said. I took his words to heart, and my creativity went into studying and surviving, into battling my emotional demons, not into expressing all of who I was.

13 Creativity doesn't go away, but we can squelch it.

Like many of us, as a young person I was drawn to crafts. I took up knitting, crocheting, even needlepoint. And while I completed some ambitious projects, I was never able to value them, to see them as worthwhile. Maybe this was because I didn't do them to express myself, but rather just to pass the time. At the same time, the warped and limited ideas I'd absorbed from my family and teachers helped me belittle those efforts. They weren't perfect. I couldn't sell them. I was not an artist. My formed creativity got more discouraged and more repressed. I think this happens to a lot of us.

14 Creativity can come out sideways.

This does not mean I was not creative. I was. I was a good student in high school and college. I was a good worker at my jobs. I was a good problem-solver. But as I moved into adulthood, those things were not meaningful enough for me. And for all the complicated reasons that are familiar to many of us, I began to drink.

For the next 20 years, a great deal of my creativity went into drinking. That may sound strange: alcoholism as a creative undertaking. But my drinking was. I'm not talking about inventing new umbrella drinks or organizing drinking contests. I'm talking about the creative energy it takes to drink all the time and still function in life. I used my creativity to live my life in a state of drunkenness. I drank every day and sometimes all day. During this time I went to graduate school and got a PhD. I taught hundreds of classes to university students. I directed a community college program for refugees. I had relationships with friends and lovers. Those were good things, but it took extra energy and cleverness to do them drunk.

Then there was maintaining my drinking habit. It took creativity to figure out how to make sure there was always enough to drink, to figure out how to dispose of the empties or deal with the blackout from the night before. What had I said and done? What damage did I need to repair?

Mostly, I used my creativity to lie, to myself and others. I convinced myself it was okay that my partner had other women and I washed down my jealousy with more bourbon. I pretended to be sober when I was anything but. And I hid from everyone the fact that alcohol was making me increasingly ill, mentally and physically. Some of my creativity went into giving acting performances. I was a great pretender.

15 Creativity may help us survive.

As I look back, all those strivings seem a pathetic way to use my creativity. But at the time, it was all I could do. I was in the grip of alcoholism and I didn't know any way out. (When I got sober in 1989, 12-Step programs and treatment centers weren't common knowledge as they are today.) So I had to keep drinking and going to work and driving carefully (both drunk and hung-over) and negotiating relationships with my family and my boyfriend and my coworkers, all the while completely impaired. My creativity helped me do that.

And I survived and went into a treatment center and began to get sober. Many things may have contributed to my survival. I know now that creativity was one of them and I am grateful.

16 After sobriety, then what?

In early sobriety, we mostly spend our time learning new responses to life and not drinking, going to meetings, working the Steps, living life in as low key a way as possible to reduce stress and anxiety. We do therapy, resurrect a work life, make amends with family. But the restlessness doesn't always go away. I went back to sugar as my fastest and surest way to take care of myself. I knew something else was going on, something was still missing, but I didn't know what.

I did a lot of service work, but I remained anxious and fidgety. I discovered Buddhism as a spiritual path and learned to accept my anxiety and my restlessness, but I still wasn't satisfied. I began to assume I never would be. I didn't necessarily want a different job or more money or another boyfriend or even more sex. But I wanted something and I didn't know what it was, and I read and I read and I couldn't figure it out, and being drunk hadn't worked and now eating a ton of sugar wasn't working either.

17 Creativity in sobriety: *available* creativity

I did not yet know then what I do now about creativity: in addition to *original* creativity and *formed* creativity, there is a third kind, ***available creativity***, and that in active addiction, I had used it to survive, and in sobriety I could use it to be more at peace.

Available creativity is the courage and willingness to try new things, and most alcoholics and addicts in recovery are blessed with a great deal of this. Otherwise, long-term sobriety would be nearly impossible. For getting sober is hard work, and staying sober even harder.

Creativity began to happen to me without me even realizing it. But I didn't yet know that my need for life to be meaningful was part of the puzzle.

18 Meaning as the missing piece

In his book, *Natural Psychology*, psychologist and creativity coach Eric Maisel says that some of us have a heightened relationship with *meaning*. Lots of people go through life and they are seldom if ever curious about what life means. For them, life just is, and they go about living that life—going to school, going to work, raising their kids—without being in a conversation about meaning. Others of us want to know what life means, sometimes desperately. I think this is a very plausible description of the hole in the soul some of us feel, of our restlessness and anxiety.

Somehow I knew all along there was something I was missing, that that sense of satisfaction, of the meaningful was possible. But I couldn't figure out how to get it and I drank to not care that it was missing. Now, after some years sober, I began to wonder. What if my addictive behaviors weren't just an escape from my painful childhood and unhappy relationships with men? What if my addiction wasn't only genetic, wasn't just a physical response to alcohol that affected 10% of the population who, like me, couldn't stop once they started? What if it was also a response to a frustrated search to have life be meaningful?

This idea began to intrigue me.

Sober Play

Sober Play suggestions are a chance to do something creative right now. They're easy, simple, and fun. In Part VI, you'll find a recap of the full *Sober Play* activities list, suggested materials for the artmaking experiences, and ways to take these exercises deeper.

WRITING

- Spend a few minutes with a family photo album and choose a photo of a person whose face intrigues you. It may be of a relative you don't know well or at all, it may be of an old friend, it may be of someone loved and lost. Write a letter from that person to you and a letter back from you (make up any details you need).
- Open a drawer in your bathroom and take out any three objects. Write a conversation between the objects in which they discuss you.
- "When Sally opened the door, a very tiny man stood there holding a very large duck." Write a one-page story that starts with this sentence.

ARTMAKING

- Make something ugly! Challenge yourself to make something really UGLY! Choose only the ugliest colors of crayons and draw only the ugliest things. Glue down cut-out shapes or collage images that will make it even more hideous. Then ask yourself, "What would make this even uglier?" Have fun with this!
- Make a collage self-portrait by piecing together images that represent different parts of who you were, who you are, and who you want to be. It doesn't have to look like a person: it's just a collection of images that represent who you are.
- Make an ink blot critter. Using watercolors or thin tempera paints, dribble several colors of paint on a piece of paper. Before the paint dries, fold the paper in quarters. Then open it up and let it dry flat. Once it's dry, find crazy animals or creatures in the paint, just like you would find characters in the clouds. Use a pen, pencil, or even crayons to outline the animals, flesh out the shapes (real or imaginary), and add details like eyes, fangs, or whiskers.

Part II
Creativity and Recovery

Out of chaos and uncertainty, the creative person concerns himself with making a meaningful life.

—Pamela K. Metz, *The Creative Tao*

1 Creativity as process

One of the benefits of practicing creative self-expression (aka artmaking in some form) is that it is often a rich and meaningful experience of process. As I write this, my mind and heart are engaged in a number of activities. Choosing the next ideas from among many, choosing the words to express them, organizing them, crafting them. It's a process I've grown accustomed to as a writer and it is usually invisible to me.

Similarly when I paint, I make dozens of small decisions in each minute: color, stroke, placement, to smudge or keep sharp, juxtaposition of line and shape. I zoom in and pan out for different perspectives on the image or the paragraph. It's a complex process, but when I let go of thinking about the complexity and just do it, my mind is fully engaged, and my anxiety and restlessness and boredom slip away.

2 Recovery as process

Learning to be comfortable in process is a good thing for those of us in recovery. When I drank, I drank to get numb. I wanted to get as far away from the process of living my life as I could because that process felt unbearable. But when we get sober, we have to be in the process all our waking hours. This, I think, is one of the true meanings of "one day at a time." Not only do we not drink or use one day at a time, but we are asked to be in our lives one day, one minute at a time. We are asked to stay in the process.

For that's what recovery is—a process, and a complex one. There is no product, no being done with recovery. We stay in it, and we make choices, both conscious and unconscious. We observe it and we do it. Immersing myself in writing and painting as processes has made recovery easier and richer for me.

My friend Lindy Fox often says that every day in recovery, we have a choice to make. We can choose to be well or we can choose to be sick and crazy. Part of being well for me is choosing to do something creative.

3 Grace in the creative process

Early this week, I had an amazing experience at the studio. I'd been struggling with a cold for a few days and had pretty low energy. But I had left a painting not quite finished and wanted to complete it. I knew that it wouldn't take too long so down to the studio I went. The building was quiet (my studio is a coop where 22 artists work), and I put on my iPod and settled into reds and pale yellows. In a half-hour, I was finished. It wasn't one of my best but it had some good moments.

I hated to leave. I had at least an hour more that I could be there, but I didn't feel up to starting another big piece. So I cast around for something to do.

In the opening chapter of my first novel, which I finished a few years ago, the main character is watching his best friend orchestrate the weaving of yards of colored silk into a split-rail fence. For the last couple of years, I've wanted to paint something I could use on the cover of the novel if I ever self-published it. But the dozen efforts I'd made so far had been pretty awful. I just couldn't get the fence to look right, let alone weave the colors in.

A few days before I'd found a website for a fence company in North Carolina. The fence and the forest looked a bit more like what I had envisioned, so I downloaded a couple of the photos. Now in the studio, I pulled them out and got some colored pencils and a big scrap of paper and began playing with drawing the fence from the photo. Again, the first effort was unsatisfying. But I didn't feel disheartened. I was in a light mood and happy to just be in process, so I turned the paper over and got out some harder pastels I don't use often and tried again. This time, somehow, I just knew how to draw the fence. It wasn't something I figured out. It was a knowing that descended on me.

And I relaxed into it and I knew I needed to do a third drawing and this time on black paper. So I scrounged around and found the only black thing I had, the backing off a pad of drawing paper, and I redid the drawing in about 10 minutes. It was perfect—just what I had wanted. Being willing to go with and stay in the process manifested a product I couldn't get when I tried for it. I call this *grace*.

4 The grace of sobriety

The spiritual experience of grace was not evident to me until I'd been sober a few years. When I first heard the saying "There but for the grace of God..." in meetings, I heard it as gratitude that my drinking life had been no worse than it was. Gratitude that I hadn't killed anybody driving drunk or ruined my health or had children who had suffered from my numbed feelings and bad choices.

It took me a while to understand that my own actions weren't the only thing keeping me sober. I learned that out of the 20 people in my treatment group, only two of us were still sober at the end of a year, a sad 10% statistic that continues to prove true about those who enter recovery. Knowing this didn't make me feel special or proud of myself. It made me curious.

I know that my intelligence didn't get me sober. I've been blessed with a good amount of smarts and have always been a good student and a quick thinker. But all of that was no match for alcohol, which, as we know, is "cunning, baffling, and powerful." I could not think myself sober any more than I could will myself sober.

I found out years after I "graduated" from the treatment center that the staff there had a pool on me. They'd had college professors come through treatment before and the longest any of them had lasted was a week. The staff were sure I'd follow suit. Professors apparently believed they were smarter than the other patients, smarter than the counselors. Elitism, snobbery—that's what the staff believed. But I think it was fear. These other academics had gotten themselves into a place where the intelligence they counted on was of no help. Only courage and willingness were going to be of any use, and my guess is they weren't sure how to call on those. *Exactly*

I stuck out the 28 days. I now know this acceptance, this persistence was grace.

5 Courage and willingness are key to both processes

Courage and willingness are probably the two most important things in the sobriety tool-kit. The courage to change and the willingness to find another way. And to keep finding another way, not just once and for all but one day at a time. Recovery is a long-term apprenticeship. We don't *get* recovered. We are *in* recovery, continually learning how to create a life that supports sobriety. Process, not product. Progress, not perfection.

Courage and willingness are also essential tools in creative self-expression. The courage to learn about the medium of expression that we've been called to or have chosen. The willingness to show up to the computer screen, to the musical instrument, to the canvas, to the garden, to the potter's wheel, and play. The courage to try new things, to keep expanding our repertoire of skills and possibilities. The willingness to move through periods of discouragement, of boredom, of emotional discomfort, and keep showing up.

A great deal of creative self-expression is showing up to the work. A great deal of sobriety is showing up for life instead of turning away.

6 Full creative self-expression

When we show up regularly to meetings, to phone calls with our sponsor or sponsees, to daily meditation and prayer, these activities become habits, good habits. Our recovery goes deeper and becomes more solid, something we can count on to sustain us when times get tough.

Similarly, when we show up regularly to our creative practice, when we go to dance group or sit down at that latest short story or spend some time every day at our collage table or drawing board, creating and making become habits, good habits. We honor our need for fun, for meaning, for joy, and that enhances and supports our recovery.

Full creative self-expression: The regular and sustained practice of creating and making for personal enrichment, fulfillment, and joy.

7 Focus on process and practice, not product

Creative self-expression is a process and a practice, not a product. There may be tangible products as a result: paintings, poems, pots. Songs and CDs, flower arrangements for a wedding, a delicious meal for friends. Showing off on the dance floor or winning a contest or an award. But these are secondary to the practice, the doing. For it is in the doing that creative self-expression happens just as it is in the doing that recovery from addiction happens.

We live in a culture that honors the product far more than the process. We buy and sell products. Production keeps our economy going. But a focus on product is not particularly helpful to the recovering addict. Product focus breeds anxiety, and most of us already have more than enough of that.

But if we give ourselves a chance to practice our art, we begin to find a level of engagement that is soothing, that is satisfying, and that supports sobriety.

8 The ordinariness of life before sobriety

Much of my young adulthood, I railed against the ordinariness of life. It wasn't an ego-driven thing. I didn't think I was special and that life ought to treat me that way. I just somehow knew that there was more to the world than I could get my hands on. There were experiences of excitement and engagement and contentment that I couldn't seem to find or figure out how to create. If I did stumble upon them, I couldn't make them last.

I went to college expecting that extraordinariness to happen there and it didn't. I went to Europe to study and expected it to happen there and it didn't. I moved into my 20s thinking that working in the world or graduate school or a steady boyfriend or living with my lover would be the answer and it wasn't. So I gave up and moved into the bottle, where the conversation about an extraordinary, meaningful life disappeared in a haze of drunkenness and self-loathing that kept me occupied for many years.

9 The ordinariness of life continues into sobriety

When I got sober, the ordinariness of the world and of life was still there, of course, only now I was in it 24/7 with no anesthetic, no alcoholic haze to soften the edges. And I didn't know what to do with myself.

Like many of us in early recovery, I sought other ways to get numb. I threw myself into meetings and service work. I went to two meetings a day, sometimes three. I went to the movies a lot, a safe place where I wouldn't drink. I jogged and ran and walked endless hours. Then late in my first year, I moved to a new town and a new teaching job and I threw myself into my work. I became the academic scholar I had been too drunk to be before. I created elaborate classroom activities, served on every committee that would have me. I still did a meeting every day, I worked the Steps with a sponsor, I began to sponsor other women. I found a 12-Step therapist and began to heal up my past.

But the nagging sense of something missing went on plaguing me, and I used sugar and other comfort foods to tamp them down.

10 Becoming a seeker

In this time of seeking, I began to read self-help books, especially those with a spiritual bent. Through a meditation tape from Shirley MacLaine, I discovered the chakras, ancient energy centers in the body. I began studying Buddhism and was deeply influenced by Kevin Griffin's *One Breath at a Time*, a discussion of the similarities between Buddhist principles and the 12 Steps. I began to develop my own meditation practice and to come to my own understanding of the Higher Power.

But again the nagging sense of something missing, a need for some more tangible connection to my inner self, continued to gnaw at me.

11 There are no simple answers, no simple solutions

We are complex beings. No one thing leads us to drinking. No one thing leads us into sobriety and keeps us coming back. And sometimes we wish there were. Perhaps that is the "easier, softer way" that the Big Book talks about, or we wish it was. One simple thing that we could do to guarantee sobriety, to guarantee contentment, to guarantee freedom and ease.

In the 23 years I have been sober, I have often wished for some one thing that would fix whatever is missing in me, all the while knowing recovery doesn't work that way. That there is no cure, not just for alcoholism, but also for my hunger for meaning. Satisfying that hunger, I've learned, is another one-day-at-a-time process.

12 Meaning lies within us, not outside of us

One of the most important ideas for me from the teachings of Eric Maisel is that meaning isn't outside of us. In the same way, any good therapist will tell you the answers to your dilemmas lie inside you. We can read self-help books and the Bible, we can follow teachers consciously or slavishly. But in the end, we must each find our own truth, decide on our own values, create our own solutions.

This is actually good news, for it gives us some control over our relationship with the meaningful. And control is a big issue for many of us. As our drinking progresses, it grows out of our control. And the more that happens, the more some of us try to control everything else. We can't control much of anything, of course, but we keep trying until that moment of surrender, of admitting we are powerless and that our lives are unmanageable.

In sobriety, I don't have the same illusions about control any more. Now I am concerned about participating in my life and having an active say in what happens to me.

Maisel asks: Where do you want to invest meaning? Where do you want to make meaning happen? Realizing that meaning-making was up to me was a great thing. I didn't have to wait for it to come to me to have it happen to me. I could actively participate in creating the experience of meaningfulness in my life.

13 What meaningful feels like

What does meaning(ful) feel like? I can't say for anyone but me. In me, it's a sense of completeness, of satisfaction, of being filled, of perfection. Perfection literally means completion. Nothing more is needed.

I feel this way often after I go to a meeting. And I feel it sometimes after an intimate conversation with a good friend, or reading a really good novel, or listening to favorite music. But I feel it most reliably when I spend time in the studio or when I write first thing in the morning. I forget about work and the worries of the world; I even forget about food!

Some people call this *being in the flow of the Universe.* Moving into a space where time disappears and we get lost in the process. Because I am a chronic hyper-vigilant, that doesn't much happen to me. I'm still conscious of time and my surroundings. But I'm happy and that is a flow of its own.

14 Meaning-making as an antidote to ordinariness

Coming into a new relationship with meaning, experiencing it as an active process rather than a passive occurrence, has made a huge difference in my life. It is my choice to decide what is meaningful for me. It is my choice to decide what is satisfying. I can take on creating a life that is rich and meaningful and no one can say different. I can fill the hole in my soul in ways that work for me.

Having control over my own meaning-making gives me a whole range of antidotes to the ordinariness of life and my dissatisfaction with it. Eric Maisel says, "Art makes you feel alive...the process of artmaking buffers you against the ordinariness of the world." I couldn't have said it better.

15 Meaning-making can happen anytime, anywhere we choose

We can invest meaning anywhere. In a conversation with a loved one. In our work. In our 12-Step service. In making amends. In prayer and meditation. In time spent in nature or at an art museum or in therapy. And we can invest it in creative self-expression, in making art.

Making art means many things to me. Collage. Drawing with colored pencils. Painting with pastels. Making dinner for friends. Taking care of the potted plants on my terrace. Taking a trip to the Yarn Garden with its luscious colors and textures. Going to the farmers market. Hosting a circle of women writers. Arranging a retreat for other creatives. Writing in my journal. Writing on a novel. Writing this sentence.

What might making art mean to you?

16 Making art, making ourselves proud

One of the most critical pieces of recovery from addiction is a renewed sense of self-worth. Gripped for years or decades by something we had no power over, something that continually humiliated us and made us hate and loathe ourselves, finding something to feel proud of is vital. Many groups celebrate milestones in recovery, recognizing that recovery is an arduous journey and lengthening our number of one days at a time is something to be proud of.

Eric Maisel acknowledges that making ourselves proud is a fundamental human characteristic. The kind of survival that we alcoholics and addicts know in our using years doesn't make us proud. But recovery does. And so can creative self-expression. Committing ourselves to an artmaking practice, to growing a flower garden, creating a cookbook of family recipes, writing stories about our life, painting or making pots, all of these positive efforts contribute to making us proud.

17 Making art can be sacred

Many great artists have seen art making as their spiritual calling, their gift to God. While I am reluctant to claim that for myself, I do experience writing and painting as sacred time.

Some of us in recovery found it easy to realign ourselves with our childhood religion when we got sober. Others of us couldn't do that or had no childhood religion to return to. We may have struggled with the "God" part of the 12 Steps. My own "as I understand God" was slow in coming and continues to evolve.

I have long been attracted to the Buddhist principles of living, which in my own simple formula boils down to doing the next right thing. And I believe that Something created us, Something brought each of us and all the rest of the world and the many universes into being. Whether there is a grand purpose in life or not, I am one of those wanting to understand the meaning of this opportunity to be alive in this time. And making art helps me do that. I hope it can do that for you as well.

Sober Play

WRITING

- Pick one of these words—*from, that, can, might*—and write an 8-line poem where the end of each line rhymes with that word.
- Pick a novel off your shelf and open to a page that has dialog. Pick any line of dialog and write a page of the beginning of a story that uses that line somehow.
- Write two different paragraphs that start with same first five words. They two can be variations on one idea or completely different from each other.

ARTMAKING

- Do a hand dance. Listen to music and move a pencil across a paper in response to the music. Don't look at the doodle; just move the pencil for 30 seconds. When the time is up, move to a new sheet of paper. When the music is over, look at your doodles. Pick your favorite and add to the doodle with watercolors or colored pencils. Try filling in the spaces with patterns.
- Connect the dots. Draw 50 dots on a page. Now, begin connecting those dots with straight lines. Use any order; just make sure all the dots are connected to at least one other dot. Use the doodle as a basis for coloring or creating patterns.
- Work on an illuminated manuscript. Turn to a random page in a book, and pick your five favorite words from the page. Then find collage images or draw pictures that somehow illuminate or illustrate the word or words. They can be on separate paper or combine to make something interesting. Include the five words in some way if you like.

Part III
Creativity and the 12 Steps

There are three guideposts to consider for creativity:
Openness, not judging, playfulness.

—Pamela K. Metz, *The Creative Tao*

THE VALUES OF CREATIVITY AND THE
VALUES OF RECOVERY

Last February, I got introduced to a set of 12 values or principles linked to the 12 Steps. And as I read through them, I was struck by their direct link to creativity.

- Honesty
- Hope
- Faith
- Courage
- Integrity
- Willingness
- Humility
- Love for others
- Justice
- Perseverance
- Spiritual awareness
- Service

What follows is a discussion of each of these life principles, their relationship to creative self-expression in general and then to a particular form or forms of expression, and some ideas on how to get started.

HONESTY

TELLING OUR OWN STORIES

It takes considerable honesty to admit we are powerless over alcohol or drugs or food or any of the other addictive substances and activities that we use to soothe our restlessness and ease our troubled minds and spirits. By the time many of us get into recovery, we are chronic liars. We've lived in denial of the depth of our misery and shame, the depth of our despair.

It can take a good while to dismantle those habits of untruth. They say in the program that it takes a month for every year of drinking to heal the body. It may take as long for us to un-learn dishonesty and develop an honest approach to life.

JOURNALING

For 20 years, I've done daily journaling, "morning pages" as Julia Cameron recommends in the *Artist's Way* program. In the early years of sobriety, doing this was a big step forward in honesty for me. It takes trust to become honest. For most of my life, I believed that the people around me didn't want to know what I was feeling. I believed that sharing my feelings was a burden to others, the way it had seemed to be a burden to my parents. I believed that "fine" was the only acceptable answer to "How are you?"

But in the journal, whose only reader was me, I could begin to sort out how I really was, what I really felt, even and especially if I wasn't sure. Each morning I could write about how I was feeling, both physically and emotionally, in as much detail as I wanted to share with myself. I could write about the events of the day before and how I felt about them. I could write about what was coming up that day and how I felt about those events and challenges. I could begin to understand, little by little, the feelings I'd been numbing out for so long.

Getting started with journaling

Morning pages
- Get a notebook or blank journal that appeals to you. If writing in something fancy intimidates you, get a simple spiral notebook.
- Get a pen that you like writing with. This is important because it should be fun, even comforting, to move the pen across the paper.*
- Arrange 15-20 minutes in your morning schedule every day. It's best to do this as close to getting up as you can. I feed my cats, brush my teeth, make tea, and sit down to write. Set a timer if you are worried about losing track of time.
- Then just write. Write whatever is on your mind, whatever is in your heart. Write quickly. Write in words, phrases, or sentences. Write in paragraphs or not.
- No need to edit, to check spelling or grammar. Who cares? No one is going to read this, maybe not even you. Remember this is not about product, it's about process.
- Fill up three pages if you can or as much as you can.
- Put your notebook in a safe place. This is for your eyes only.
- Do this every day. It will make a world of difference.

If you use the computer a lot, it is important to do the morning pages by hand. The physical act is very different; it is slower and soothing. Trust me on this.

REFLECTIVE JOURNALING

There are many things you can do in your journal. *Reflective journaling* is one. In this creative practice, instead of writing whatever is going on with you, you write on a topic of your choosing. If you've ever done extensive writing on each of the 12 Steps with a sponsor or a group, you've done reflective journaling. (Much of the writing in this book came from my own reflective journaling.)

Like Morning Pages, reflective journaling is not a formal writing process or meant to be shared. These are your thoughts on subjects of interest to you, subjects that could include marriage, parenting, bosses, working for a living, sobriety, gratitude, everything and anything.

Your reflective journaling may include your experiences and your dreams, your anger and your joy. It's a great way to get clear about what's important to you. It can be an occasional thing or a committed practice. Like most creative activities, it will be most meaningful and satisfying if you make it a regular part of your life.

Getting started with reflective journaling

- Decide on a journal, notebook, or computer file that will hold your reflective journaling. Some people like to keep just one journal for both morning pages and reflective journaling. I like having two different journals. Some people hand-write morning pages (recommended) but then use the computer for their reflective work.
- Set a timer (30 minutes is a good amount but 15 minutes will do).
- Just start writing. You can continue where you left off the last time or start a new idea. I like to write on the same topic for a while, usually a month. And I like to have a list of ongoing topics in the front of my reflective journal so that I don't lack for ideas. The 12 values listed above might be a great place to start. There's easily a year's worth of reflective journaling there.

REFLECTIVE JOURNALING WITH A GROUP

Reflective journaling with a group of others who are writing on the same topics can be a wonderful experience. When we get sober, most of us have to learn how to be social in a different way. Without the lubricant of alcohol, many of us find ordinary conversation too ordinary. Again, we want something more meaningful. Reflective journaling is a great way into more meaningful conversations.

Getting started with reflective journaling in a group

- Groups typically meet every two weeks or once a month. Meeting for two hours is a good amount of time. A group of 4-6 members is a good number.
- While it may seem a good idea to rotate where the group meets, it usually proves simpler to pick one home and meet there each time. The group leader can change each time though.
- I don't recommend serving food but having tea or coffee and water available is a nice gesture.
- During the time between group sessions, members commit to writing a certain number of times on the same topic.
- Group sessions might start with a short silent meditation, then a 5-minute free writing on a "prompt" (usually a sentence or phrase or perhaps a quote) proposed by the host.
- When the timer goes off, each person reads their response to the prompt. Usually there are no comments.
- Next, members each read one of their reflective journaling entries written before the group meeting.
- After each group member has read, discussion begins. Some groups limit the time of discussion; others let the discussion run its course. Discussion focuses on the content of the writing, NOT its form (such as vocabulary or grammar or style).
- In closing, members choose a new topic or agree to stay on the same one and then each commit to the number of times that they will journal before the next session.

A word about critique groups.

Reflective journaling groups, like memoir groups below, are not critique groups. Critique groups are a long-standing writers' tradition in which group members listen and comment critically on each member's writing with the purpose of helping that member move towards publication. It takes a tough skin to weather this kind of response to our work. I encourage you to find a *support* group of other writers, not a *critique* group.

USING PROMPTS FOR INSPIRATION

The practice of writing prompts can be a natural extension of journaling. Prompts are timed writings (I've found 10 minutes is a good length) based on a word or a phrase. These can be reflective writings, experiences from your life, or made-up stories about made-up characters (what we call *fiction*).

When I first started writing prompts, I let whatever wanted to be written come up. They were a more structured form of journaling and I would write about memories or things that had come up on my 4th Step list. They served to help me increase my honesty and my ability to reflect on events and ideas.

Many writing circles use the prompt idea for an opening activity. After a few moments of meditation, the group settles in to write for 10 minutes on a prompt given by the host. Then each member reads their response to the prompt. There's generally no commentary afterwards.

Later, after I'd written a bunch of prompts, I began to make them fictional by introducing the name of a character in the very first sentence and then seeing where it would go, how the story would develop. These fictional prompts also taught me a lot about what was of concern to me: relationships with my parents, my friends, my dreams and hopes.

People who choose writing as a practice of creative self-expression will often use prompts to improve their skills and to become more at ease with writing and making stuff up. That's what happened for me. After I wrote my memoir,

I wanted to see if I could write fiction and writing prompts was a really low-stress way to do that. One month every prompt was written about Allison, a girl I knew in first grade (and have never seen since). And my friend Pam Stringer is using prompts to imagine characters for a novel she'd like to write about a small town in Oklahoma.

Don't be surprised if some pretty weird and wonderful stories start to surface. They're just waiting there inside of all of us.

A wonderful source of prompts and encouragement is Judy Reeves' *The Writer's Book of Days*. Judy is funny, helpful, and encouraging, and her book has hundreds of prompts.

Getting started with writing prompts

- Decide whether you are going to write your prompts in a notebook or a computer file. I use a notebook that's especially for prompts.
- Set a timer for 10 minutes.
- Write the prompt at the top of the page (and the date, if you like).
- Write whatever comes up. Don't edit, don't worry about grammar or spelling, don't worry if it's a complete story. Just write whatever gets prompted.
- If you're interested in writing fictional prompts, include the name of a character in the first sentence and write the prompt about them. For example, if the prompt is "red teacup," a possible opening sentence might be this: "Madeline threw the red teacup at the refrigerator." Then go on from there.
- When the timer goes off, finish the sentence and stop. If the "story" isn't finished, don't worry about it. You can always come back to it later. But don't do that the next day. The next day, write another prompt.

Note: I've included a starter list of prompts in Section VI.

CREATIVITY AND THE 12 STEPS: HONESTY

Admitting we are powerless

Making art is one of the few times I consciously acknowledge that I am not in control of the outcome. This doesn't mean that I've lost the ability to make decisions about what I'm making or the ability to take action on those decisions. It means that I'm being honest with myself.

Engaging in something creative means admitting that I don't know. I don't know what the finished product will look like. I don't know what the next "right" or "perfect" step is. I'm creating something that hasn't been there before, so of course I don't know.

I'm not in control of the outcome, only the steps I take along the way. And every color I choose, every piece of paper I glue down, every shape I draw—it may not come out as I intended. But whatever happens is a direct result of what I am, what I observe, what I do in that moment. The face I draw today may not look like a photograph or a drawing by Leonardo da Vinci. It'll look exactly like what it is: a face I drew today. And there's no way to fake it.

Yes, I am admitting that I am powerless over the outcome. But that powerlessness is not a bad thing. It's actually a relief. Sure, the not-knowing is scary, but it also means I don't have to be perfect. I can experiment, I can play, I can mess up, and I can be surprised. And that's a good thing.

—Bridget

Question: What thoughts come up when you consider letting go of how your creative project turns out?

Suggestion: Do something where you enjoy the process. This will help take the pressure off of the outcome.

HOPE

TWO SIMPLE WAYS TO PUT MORE COLOR INTO LIFE

When I got to the treatment center in 1989, I was hopeless and demoralized. I knew I was an alcoholic and had even been saying that to myself for the last two years. And I'd known for more than a decade that how I drank (in the morning, every day, all day) was abnormal. But I didn't know a way out. I had tried everything to moderate my drinking, I had tried several times to stop, but I had always gone back to it and it was always worse than before: I drank more and I was sicker, both emotionally and physically. I had no hope going into the treatment center, only desperation. I was so tired of being sick, of being unhappy. I was willing to be restored to sanity.

I did not have a happily-ever-after experience with rehab. I did not find those 28 days a hopeful experience. I did begin to feel better physically and there was a lot of talk about how if I went to meetings and worked the Steps, I wouldn't have to drink again. But I didn't really believe it. All I could see stretching ahead of me were endless gray days of no anesthetic, no way to deal with the unbearable and meaningless anxiety of life and relationships. I couldn't believe that a meeting once a day was going to cure my chronic state of being restless, irritable, and discontent. Then I discovered coloring.

COLORING—YUP, GOOD OLD-FASHIONED COLORING

During a visit to a friend in Richmond, Virginia, in my second year of sobriety, a trip to a toy store to get a gift for my 2-year-old nephew changed my life. Over in a corner, I found a set of posters in black and white that came with colored markers. The posters were of African village scenes and they were very cool. And I decided to get one and color it for my nephew's room. For the next several months, I spent my lonely sober weekends coloring the whole series of posters. They were intricate enough to satisfy my love of detail and the images were playful enough to just be fun. I bought more markers to have a wider range of colors to play with.

I found coloring to be an amazingly meditative and relaxing activity. It was a healthy way to fill up some of the time I used to spend drinking, and some of the terrible restlessness of early sobriety began to leave me. At the time, I thought of these purely as ways to pass the time. But the coloring kept me interested and soothed me in a new and welcome way.

Soothing is important to those of us in recovery. I think anxiety and our heightened response to it are one of the underlying factors in addiction. We may be more sensitive to anxiety or have a hair-trigger anxious button that goes off easily. It may be brain chemistry or a personality characteristic or something ingrained in us as children. Whatever it is, we looked to drugs and alcohol to soothe it. And now we must find something else.

There are lots of other addictions out there: work, exercise, shopping, food. We can get compulsive about just about anything if it soothes us. Artmaking in whatever form we choose may be one of the healthiest choices. In early sobriety, I was terrified that I would have to live with constant anxiety. Artmaking gave me hope that that didn't have to be so.

Getting started with coloring

Coloring is an inexpensive activity that doesn't require much space or clean-up. A coloring book and a few pencils is all you need. It's easy to take with you anywhere and you'd be surprised how many people will color with you.

- Decide on coloring tools. Color crayons and colored pencils work well in coloring books. Colored markers are too wet for the soft paper of most coloring books and are better on coated paper like posters. There are a huge variety of coloring tools available in a wide range of colors and costs. Colored pencil sets can cost from a few dollars to hundreds of dollars. There are water-soluble pencils where the color will spread if you run a wet brush over the image you've colored. There are pastel pencils (soft chalk in pencil form). I started off with a simple set of 12 markers from the grocery store and 12 hard colored pencils from an office supply store.

- Equally, the range of coloring books is amazing. Dover coloring books are inexpensive and come in a wide variety of subjects: from African history to wild animals. There are also anatomy coloring books and geometric tile coloring books. Toy stores, book stores, and the Internet have a wealth of choices.

- A little more elaborate set-up involves plastic brushes that have a compartment for water and small sheets of watercolor pigment from Peerless. You can color or paint with them. When I was on a recovery speaking tour with five other women, we sat in a hotel lobby, drank tea, and painted little pictures for each other. Great fun!

- You can move into creating your own designs, your own coloring books from online images, or doing freeform drawing and art. The Zentangle kits and books are a fun way to create patterns of your own to color.

COLLAGE

Eight or nine years ago, I got introduced to collage, the art of putting glue to paper. In its simplest form, it involves finding printed images, arranging them on a background of some kind, and gluing them down. Collage was a favorite tool of painters like Picasso, Braque, Matisse, and Salvador Dali.

Any two images glued together makes a collage, but it is an endlessly fascinating form of play. Collages can be romantic or mysterious or absurd, like a bear's head on a fashion model. A collage can contain two images or dozens. Images can be cut or torn; they can be whole or partial. I have found collage to be just as soothing as coloring.

Getting started with collage

- Begin collecting images that interest you. Magazines, old art books, greeting cards, catalogs, calendars are all good sources. You will soon discover what kinds of paper you like (slick, matte, soft) and whether you like large images or small.
- Try different kinds of backing. Some people prefer to work on cardboard or poster board. Some like card stock (a little thinner but still stiff), and some like construction paper. I like working in journal type books. I have found some that have manila folder pages and spiral binding. They work well for me. I moved to working in books when the number of poster collages I was making was overwhelming my wall space. I love looking through my books.
- You can tear the images out—many collage creators like the ragged edges for the texture it brings to the image—or you can use scissors. Fiskars makes great paper-cutting scissors. I have two pair, a large one and a very sharp small pair.
- Besides images and something to stick them to, all you need is glue. There are many kinds of adhesive out there and if you really get into it, you can investigate them. I use glue sticks although I do get a more expensive kind at an art supply store as they seem to work better and hold longer.

Collaging has endless appeal for me. I like doing them in monochrome: choosing one dominant color (all yellow images or blue images). I also like to have a unifying background laid down first. You can also use markers, paints, crayons, colored pencils, words in many forms, rubber stamps, glitter on top of your collages. It's just so much fun!

A word about plagiarism and copyright.

Using other artists' work as inspiration for your paintings or as a part of your own work as in collage may be fine as long as you don't sell the work you make with it or display that work publicly. There's a long tradition of copying, borrowing, and stealing from other artists and our use of it for our private artmaking poses few problems. Note, however, my use of "may" in these sentences. What's legal, what's moral, what's right are all very hazy. There's lots of material on the Internet that discusses the controversies. If you get to a point where you want to show or display your work and it involves the images of others, you must get their permission and if you sell the work, you may owe them some money. It is best to speak with an intellectual property lawyer to be sure.

Copyright doesn't last forever so you can safely work with materials that are in the public domain. And you can ask permission. I paint from some of the photos of my photographer brother-in-law and he gives me permission to do so.

CREATIVITY AND THE 12 STEPS: HOPE

Coming to believe that a power greater than ourselves can restore us

Artmaking is all about possibilities. There are an endless number of colors, an infinite number of marks and shapes we can make, such a variety of words and sounds and textures. One reason why my darkest times seemed so dark was that I felt I had no choice: I had to drink, I had to buy that pair of earrings, I had to eat another cookie. I had deep emotional pain or anxiety, and the only option that seemed open to me was to return to a compulsive, numbing habit.

And there were times when I painted from that same place—or tried to. I'd get caught up in my fear and my desire for approval. I'd try to make something that I thought was "good" or something that I thought other people would like. I tried to use the painting to push down the anxiety that I'm not enough as I am. But there is no joy in that. So for years, I simply didn't paint.

Then I took a painting class with Stewart Cubley, co-author of *Life, Paint, & Passion*. We were given brightly colored tempera paints, a few brushes, and a piece of paper taped to a wall for a process Stewart called *process painting*. But most importantly, we were given permission. Permission to choose the color that sang to us and to dip our brush into it. Permission to put the loaded brush to paper and make whatever mark or shape we wanted to. It didn't have to look like anything. It didn't have to be good. It just needed to have some energy behind it. And that felt like hope to me.

In that moment, the permission Stewart's class offered felt like a gift from a higher power. Now, when the fear of rejection or the desire for approval comes up, I try to remember that gift. I remember the permission to pursue painting just for the joy of the making.

—Bridget

Question: What might be the gift your higher power has to offer you through your own creative self-expression?

Suggestion: Consider the creative things you loved to do as a child, and try doing a few of those things now.

FAITH

TRUSTING IN LIFE

When I got sober, I had trust in very little. I'd grown up in a family where self-reliance was a supreme virtue. And uncontrollable drinking and my inability to get out of an emotionally abusive relationship had eroded any sense I had of being in charge of my life. I didn't believe in God, I didn't believe in dreams, I didn't believe in possibility. I lived in cynicism, strongly supported by my many years of academic training, and in resignation.

As I began to gather sober days together into sober years, I began to learn to trust again. In the meetings, I saw that people who worked the Steps, who had sponsors, who kept coming to the meetings didn't drink again. They were happy and calm. I began to trust that this could be true for me too. I began to see that all the misery in my life wasn't just about me and some deep defect in me. Rather, it was about the effect of alcohol on my emotions, on my judgment, and on my body. Now that I wasn't at its mercy anymore, a different kind of life became possible. And faith became possible.

I went back to meditation after a hiatus of 20 years. I became interested in the Buddhist philosophy. I warmed to the idea of some kind of Higher Power in my life. I became teachable again.

In my community (Portland, Oregon), many artists and seekers teach workshops, both to make a little money and to share what they know or are learning. A workshop involving collage was particularly important for me.

VISION BOARDS

Vision boards are a more intentional form of collage. Most of my collage work is artistic in that my only intention is to create something pleasing to me. In a vision board, we gather images that represent the dreams and possibilities we hold for ourselves, both known to us and that may be a surprise to us.

Doing a vision board calls on our faith and belief in life, our belief that life and the future can be good for us, that our circumstances can not only change but improve. At the same time, we hold the process loosely, much as we talk in the program about doing the footwork but leaving the results to the Higher Power.

Doing a vision board in a leaderless group or with a buddy is very fun. It's fascinating to see what other people dream of. But it can also be done on your own. And it can be good to do a vision board each year at New Year's or on your sober anniversary or every five or ten years to see what's changed and what's coming up for you.

Getting started with vision boards

- Gather a lot of magazines. *O* magazine, *National Geographic*, and *Real Simple* are good choices because they have lots of diverse ads and stories with color images. I also like to go to a big bookstore or a newsstand that carries a lot of magazines and pick a few foreign magazines or ones that are new to me (be sure they have lots of images of different kinds).
- Decide how big you want to work. If you are going to put your vision board up in your home or office where you can look at it often, poster board that is 24"x24" or 24"x36" is a good size. You can buy poster board in most office supply stores, art stores, and bigger supermarkets and drugstores.
- Gather your scissors and glue sticks and any embellishments you might want to add (ribbon, glitter, markers) and a kitchen timer. Have your journal or notebook and a pen handy.
- You may also have personal photographs that you want to put on the vision board. If you have the photos on your computer, print them out on regular paper so they'll be easier to glue.
- Vision boards can be made quickly or more slowly, but they seem to work best if the time is limited. I find an uninterrupted 90 minutes is a good amount of time.
- The process is pretty simple.

Step 1: Set a timer for 20 minutes. Look through the magazines and other images you've collected and pick out or tear/cut out those that appeal to you. Don't think much; just go with your interest and desires. Maybe a picture of trekkers in the Himalayas calls to you but you don't know why. Set it aside. Maybe it's a fashion model getting out of a limo. Tear it out. Anything that calls to you is worth considering. When the timer goes off, stop no matter how many or how few images you have.

Step 2: Reset the timer for 20 minutes. Go back through the images you have selected and begin to work with them. Do you want only the comfy bed in the picture? Cut or tear it out. Do you want the beach from one picture and the sky from another? Cut or tear them from the original. Some people like working with whole pictures juxtaposed. Others, like me, want details. And I admit that I love cutting paper with sharp scissors. I loved it as a kid and I love it now. So I like to cut out smaller things (a lamp, a dog, a flower) and add them to my collage. Begin honing in on the things you want to include on your vision board. And be sure to include anything that really calls to you, even if it makes no sense with the other images. Visions aren't always logical or practical. If that cruise ship calls to you, put it in even if you can't imagine ever having the money. When the timer goes off, stop even if you aren't done sorting.

Step 3: Reset the timer for 20 minutes. It's now time to arrange the images on the board and glue them down. Most people work in one of two ways. They lay everything out in a pleasing arrangement and then glue the images all down. Or they just start gluing one image at a time and trusting that the right organization will happen. (I'm one of these latter folks. I like the surprise of what happens.) Again, I encourage you to work quickly without a lot of determination. Just do it and see what happens. When the timer goes off, stop. You can always add more images later.

Step 4: Reset the timer for 15 minutes. Find your journal and pen and write about the board in front of you. What images surprise you? What images represent long-held dreams? Is there a mood or attitude represented by the images? Do certain colors dominate? What can you learn from what you've put together?

Step 5: In the last 15 minutes, share your vision board with your buddy or group. Or just sit quietly with the images and let your mind wander. It is often good to do nothing after a creative experience.

You may wish to place your vision board somewhere in your home or office so it can remind you of the things you long for. Some people use it as an active springboard for taking steps to manifest those things. Others prefer a quieter approach in letting those things find them.

CREATIVITY AND THE 12 STEPS: FAITH

Deciding to turn our will and our lives over to the care of Spirit

When I start working on a piece, I never know how it's going to turn out. Part of the challenge and the joy of artmaking for me is that I have to trust that it will all turn out okay. I have to trust that the colors I put down are the colors that are supposed to be there—at least for now. I have to trust that even if the making is not going as I intended, the journey will lead me somewhere interesting.

Faith is a tremendous piece of the creative puzzle for me. Solutions to an assemblage (a sculpture made of found objects) will come to me when I let go and step away from wrangling with the problem. An inspiration for a painting will appear when I'm out walking or working on another piece or fixing dinner or taking a shower. And sometimes, when I'm working on a creative piece, solutions to problems in my life will also appear.

I practice letting go of the outcome and just doing the next thing. Notice I didn't say the "right" thing, just the next thing. And usually the next thing is the result of a gut feeling, an intuitive impulse. And that outcome may end up being better than anything I could have imagined. Or, frankly, it may be infinitely worse. And that's okay too. Having faith means that I can accept that *ugly* may be part of the process.

For me, the action of faith isn't a blind trust. It's part of a larger conversation with Spirit, a process that starts with listening. Faith just means trusting that the conversation will lead somewhere valuable.

—Bridget

Question: What does it mean for you to turn over the outcome of your creative expression to a higher power?

Suggestion: Some creatives find it helpful to say a prayer, meditate, or journal a bit before working on a project. They want to tap into that connection with the Higher Power as guidance. How might this look for you?

COURAGE

UNCOVERING OUR STORIES, UNCOVERING OUR FEELINGS

Each person has a story to tell.
When you know your own story,
You begin to understand your life.

—Pamela K. Metz, *The Creative Tao*

One of the integral pieces of recovery in the 12-Step tradition is telling our stories. We tell those stories so that those others can feel less alone in their shame and self-loathing. We tell them so we can understand ourselves and forgive ourselves.

We also use the 4th Step to uncover our stories, the pattern of our choices, the places where we got lost, the places where our true selves went to hide. It takes considerable courage to do this Step, to look at ourselves and our lives squarely and without blinking. But the rewards are immense. And making creative self-expression part of this process, especially in later recovery, helps us create something to be proud of out of all of that messiness.

WRITING AND TELLING YOUR OWN STORY

Story-telling is one of the most basic human creative experiences. We are born to love them and learn from them. The 12-Step programs recognized this right away; the early founders discovered that telling our stories to each other could help heal us and keep us sober. Between 2003 and 2007, I wrote my own story, which eventually became a memoir, *Sober Truths: The Making of an Honest Woman*. It began as a collection of stories and turned into an extraordinary experience of coming to "not regret the past nor wish to shut the door on it."

For some of us, there can be a natural progression from writing morning pages to more reflective journaling to writing stories from our past, both the good and the painful. Writing a memoir can be a fruitful practice for many of us in recovery. It is not about publication although you may decide to do that, like I did. It is about exploring our past, our patterns, our choices and decisions, and making something creative out of them: putting those experiences to good use.

Many memoirs start out as a collection of detailed scenes that are then put together into a coherent whole when you find a theme that unites some or all of the stories. I wrote about 60 scenes. It wasn't until I finished them and was polishing the writing that I realized the most important theme in them was honesty, that my memoir was about how I learned to be dishonest as a child and young adult and how I had to learn to be honest as a recovering person. Once I saw that, I knew how to organize the stories (the first half is chronological until I get sober and the second half is grouped around parts of my life, like spirituality, creativity, relationships, family). I also knew which scenes to let go of—all those that didn't relate to honesty/dishonesty. I ended up with 28 stories.

Memoir writing is another creative practice that can be done solo or in a group. A once-a-month group, conducted along the lines of a reflective journaling group, can be a wonderful support in this process. Each group member agrees to write one story from their experience, either using a theme as in reflective journaling or an incident from their list of personal experiences. Those stories are read to each other at the group. Again, this is not a critique group but a gathering of quiet and supportive listeners.

Getting started writing memoir stories

- Make a list of pivotal moments in your life, moments in which you made a decision, whether conscious or unconscious, that impacted the direction your life took. This can be an ongoing list that you add to as memories return. Some of these will be big decisions but some may seem quite small. Don't reject those small events; just add them to the list. Here are some of the stories that were on my list:
  - Starting to eat chocolate that I hid in my desk in 5th grade
  - Deciding to stay with my lover after I found out he was seeing other women
  - Going to my first painting workshop
  - Going to my first silent meditation retreat
  - The day I decided to go into rehab
  - My first 12-Step meeting
  - The first time a man hit me
  - The first time I got drunk
  - The moment I learned that my parents had had a child who died
- Pick a story from the list and begin working on it as a scene. A scene covers a distinct period of time. My memoir opens with a scene of me in the doctor's office, and it describes those 25 minutes of my admitting my alcoholism and agreeing to go to treatment.
- Telling the story in present tense (I am sitting) instead of past tense (I was sitting) will make for a more immediate experience for the reader or listener. But past tense is fine too. Example of the opening of a scene in present tense:

  I am sitting on the examining table of my doctor's office. The air conditioning is on, but I am sweating as if I've just run a mile. I use the green paper gown to mop up the sweat. My head pounds but that is nothing new. I feel like I will throw up at any minute, but that is also nothing new. I am hoping the doctor will give me a prescription for Valium, so I can detox myself. I have been drunk for the last month.

- The idea of scene is important. Most of your listeners and readers will be as accustomed to TV and the movies as you are. As we read, we create little movies in our heads. For many of us, our memories also play out as movies in our heads. So writing in a way that encourages your listener or reader to envision your story as scene will be helpful.

- Be sure to add sensory details to your scene: colors, smells, sounds, touch, taste. You want the reader to experience your experience with you. Not every scene has to have a lot of sensory detail but we experience through the body, not just through the eyes and the mind.
- Use direct speech (dialog) whenever possible to convey important information. Instead of *He told me he was leaving*, use *"I'm leaving," he said.*

A word about giving feedback in a writing group.

In a memoir support group, respect and kindness prevail. Our writings, like all things we create, are dear to us. We often put our tenderest selves into the work. The writing groups I lead make only two kinds of suggestions as feedback. These suggestions are extremely helpful to the writer and are respectful of the writer's fragile creative self. Here are the two things we comment on:

- Where in the story I wanted to hear more.
- Where in the story I got lost or confused.

WRITING POETRY

Writing memoir is a way of uncovering not only our stories but also uncovering our feelings about those experiences. Poetry is a long-standing form of creativity for expressing feelings. The basis of most poetry is our life experiences, our stories, our choices. It's just the form that is different. I'd never written much poetry, but last year, a local poet was offering an inexpensive and low-key online class to write a poem a day for a month. Quality was not a requirement, she said, just the doing. My kind of creative endeavor! I took that challenge and had so much fun that I went on to write many more poems last year, and a few of them I really liked.

Many colleges, community colleges, and community writing associations offer classes in poetry writing. But if you're a beginner, I don't recommend them. Here's why. Our creative selves are fragile. It doesn't take much to discourage us. An unkind word from an oblivious teacher, a cruel word from a competitive fellow student, a brilliant poem from a well-experienced poet who shouldn't even be in the class, all these can devastate us. We need to build up some experience, some resilience, and some creative toughness before we subject ourselves to that.

In the 1990s, I took a short story class from a teacher I hadn't heard of. I stuck it out but got very discouraged. It was a critique class and she had a couple of favorite students who got most of her attention. And she saw her role not as encouraging us but as improving us. I didn't write again for five years. When I took that online poetry class two years ago, we had a chance every day to post our poem for others to read and comment on. I'd learned my lesson and I didn't post until late in the month. I waited to see what kinds of comments others made (they turned out to be gentle and encouraging) and when I felt safe, I stuck my toe in the water and posted some of mine.

So it's important to protect your creative self from unkindness and unwanted suggestions. There are other good ways to start writing poetry besides taking a class.

But wait, you say. *I don't know anything about writing poetry. Shouldn't I read a bunch first? What about things like rhyme and meter and form? Don't I have to worry about that stuff?*

Nope.

Like all art forms, poetry can be simple or complex. You can bring years of literary knowledge and writing experience to poetry writing, or you can bring no knowledge and experience at all. Just like drawing, which can be an elaborate studio experience with many tools or a simple pen on a scrap of paper. Or singing, which can be a public performance after years of training or a simple song as you do the dishes. That's the beauty of creative self-expression as a pastime. You don't need to be great or skilled to do it and have fun. Anybody can dance or paint or write poetry. I wish everybody would.

But to give you a simplistic definition, poetry is writing that is not prose. This paragraph is *prose*. It has the form of sentences grouped together in a paragraph. Most of the writing we encounter, from newspapers to books to letters to web screens, is in prose form. Poetry uses lines differently. Here is the same writing in a poem.

> In essence, poetry
> Is writing that is
> Not prose.
> That last paragraph is *prose*.
> Sentences grouped together.
> The writing we encounter most often
> Is prose.
> Poetry
> Uses lines differently.

My definition of poetry: Groups of selected words that capture and express a moment in time or a single experience and that use lines differently from prose. Anybody can write poetry using this definition, including you.

At the same time, there are probably a million things that you could learn about writing poetry: how to use rhyme (interior and exterior), varying line length, playing with classical forms like the sonnet or the sestina, learning about internal rhythms. Enough for a lifetime of learning and challenge and the satisfaction of mastery. As Eric Maisel says, the apprenticeship to a creative form never ends.

In fact, that idea has been of enormous support to me in both my creative self-expression and my sobriety. When things go well, I say to myself, "My apprenticeship continues." When I hit a bump or a glitch or a confrontation with a friend that I don't handle well or a poem doesn't work out well, I say to myself, "My apprenticeship continues." Simple and reassuring.

Remember too that poems can be spontaneous, that they can express what John Fox, a poetry therapist, calls "the truth of us right now." You can cultivate the urge to write poems by just jotting them down whenever they call to you. You see something of beauty, you hear a snippet of conversation that clicks your imagination into gear, you feel inexplicable joy or sadness. These are all great times to write a poem or even part of a poem.

Getting started with poetry writing

- Start to become conscious of the poetry all around you. At its heart, poetry is the use of words and images to express a thought or experience. Poetry exists in song lyrics, in advertising slogans, in the conversations of the people you interact with every day.
- Where do you hear an interesting phrase or sentence? I carry a small notebook around with me in my purse and jot down phrases I like.
- Read poetry. If you find this medium of self-expression intriguing but intimidating, start with poems for children or high school students.
- Read accessible poets. Like all art media, there are simple and complex versions. Two of my favorite accessible poets are Mary Oliver and William Carlos Williams.
- The Internet has a wealth of poetry on it. On a number of sites, you can sign up to receive a poem a day by email.
- Write a paragraph of sentences that describe something beautiful: a hike, a sunset, meeting your first grandchild, a lovely meal, a sweet memory. Then pull out phrases from that paragraph and arrange them line by line into a poem. Do that again with another memory. Do it again. You are now writing poetry.
- Write a poem about an everyday task: brushing your teeth, cleaning the litter box, taking out the garbage. See where it takes you. Write another. And another.
- Organize a small group of beginning poets with kind hearts. Write poems together from prompts. Read them aloud to each other with respect in the listening.

A word about quantity vs. quality.

Many of us get stopped in doing any kind of artmaking or creative work because of our perceptions about the quality of our products. This is perhaps the deadliest sin possible against our fragile creative selves. It may take a long time to get good (and remember you get to decide what's good). When I first started drawing, I turned out crap for two years. But I liked doing it so much, I learned to not care.

Note the "I learned" in the last sentence. Of course, I wanted to be brilliant right out of the gate. Who doesn't? But I wanted to know how to draw and since I didn't know, I had to learn. Drawing is a skill and one I didn't naturally have so I had to learn. The best way to learn? Draw a lot, sew a lot, garden a lot, cook a lot, write a lot of poems. Pick something you enjoy the doing of, the process of, and then do it a lot. You will get better. In fact, if you do it a lot, you won't be able to keep yourself from getting better.

A Poem-a-Day Challenge

- Pick a period of time that seems both doable and a stretch. A month is a great one.
- Make a list of daily prompts, things you could write poems about. You can make a list of experiences you've had, a list of your possessions (the stories behind them and why you've kept them make for wonderful poems), a list of all the places you've lived or worked, a list of all your vacations, a list of pivotal moments in the years you were drinking or using. Any list will do. I suggest you have 50 items on your list, even though months only last 28-31 days. That way you'll have lots of choices.
- Get a spiral notebook. It can be an old one or a new one, large or small. While of course you can write poetry on the computer, poetry is a sensual form of writing and is lovely to do by hand. Also your notebook will allow you to write poetry anywhere: on the bus to work, at your desk during a break, waiting for a friend in a coffee shop, on the patio in the summer mornings.
- Get a pen you really like. I'm particularly fond of Uniball pens as I like a smooth write. Others swear by ballpoints or pencils. Just get some of what you really like.

- Pick a topic from your list and go for it.
- Some people like to use a timer with poetry, say 30 minutes, but I often find I want to work on the poem all day. I'll get a start during my morning writing session, but then I'll leave the poem out where I can see it and stop by periodically during the day and read it and scratch something out or add something in the margin. Towards the end of the day, I'll type up what I have but I always hang on to the page of scribbled work.
- Start a new poem the next day and the next, even if the one from the day before is incomplete. Just keep drafting. You can always go back and rework the poems until you're more satisfied.
- Poetry prompts: Any object, any room, any plant or animal, any experience. Or read a poem by someone else, pick a line, and make it the first line of your poem.

A word about completion.

When is a poem (or a painting or a short story or a garden) finished? A piece of art is finished when you either run out of time to work on it or you run out of interest. Most poems and paintings and stories and gardens and drawings can be endlessly reworked. Each of us has to decide for ourselves when a piece is done.

The longer I paint, the more clearly I sense when a painting is done. Sometimes it happens quickly. I have color on all the places I want to have color, and I step back and look at it for a few minutes and feel satisfied. Other times, I put the piece up and continue to tinker with it for a few days, or I decide to do the same image again in a slightly different way because something doesn't feel quite right.

Sometimes when I read through a poem, I'll feel just the opposite. Not satisfied at all. Sometimes I can see right away what needs to be altered or added or deleted and sometimes I can't, so I'll put the piece away for a few days or even a month and let my subconscious work on it. Then, at some point, I'll just know that it's time to work on it again, and I'll have an answer.

Notice I didn't say *the* answer. One of the great joys of creative work is that there isn't just one answer, one possibility. There are many. This is wonderful for us folks in recovery whose lives narrowed down at the end of our active addiction to just one thing: getting more booze or drugs or food or gambling. Many of us lived for a long time in that narrow space. Instead, doing creative work is thrillingly expansive: so many possibilities and all of them right.

At the same time, cultivating a sense of completeness can be very helpful for those of us in recovery. A plaguing aspect of addiction for me was the constant sense of dissatisfaction. Just one more. Just one more drink. Just one more bowl of ice cream. Just one more new book. Just one more relationship. In my active drinking days, I never seemed to get enough. Working with artmaking, we can begin to find a sense of just right. I'm learning to look at a painting I've done and say okay, that's right just as it is. I'm learning to find where I feel completeness in my body. Where do you feel it?

CREATIVITY AND THE 12 STEPS: COURAGE

Making a searching and fearless moral inventory

Sometimes, what shows up when I'm drawing or painting is ugly. Sometimes, it's weird or dark or creepy. I've ended up with paintings covered with penises and stitched-up mouths and gaping wounds. I've made stories and performances full of dirty words and embarrassing personal details. It's tempting not to paint or write those things. We may associate art only with the beautiful, the acceptable. We may want our recovery to be just as beautiful and acceptable. But this is the Step that pushes us to acknowledge and accept all of ourselves, even the parts we may consider ugly or weird or creepy.

Many of us come into recovery with shameful pasts or carrying huge anger and resentment. Making art out of those experiences or those feelings can be a safe way to admit them, explore them, and perhaps even work through them. That's part of what art lets us do. Even if we never share those stories with another human being, art lets us acknowledge them and takes steps towards accepting them. And since we are making art primarily for ourselves, for our own satisfaction and sense of meaning (not necessarily to show or sell), we can let all parts of ourselves come out: our joy, our gratitude, our anger, our fear.

Remember we're talking here about creative *self*-expression, letting your self out, not keeping it bottled up. The wonderful thing is that there is room in our art and our creative self-expression for *all* of our unique self. There is no "correct" subject matter. There is no "correct" outcome. We just have to be brave enough to see what's in there.

—Bridget

Question: What are you most afraid will come out if you give yourself over to total creative self-expression?

Suggestion: Go and ahead and try painting or drawing or writing about the things that most scare you; there's a lot of energy in those things, and I can guarantee you won't get bored.

INTEGRITY

OWNING OUR LIVES, OWNING OUR WORDS

All of the 12 Steps are about integrity. We get honest in Step 1 and we do our best to stay honest all through our recovery. When we do a 5th Step with our sponsor or a trusted friend, we own our lives and begin to have a different relationship with our word and our feelings and how we relate to them. This is integrity in action and in being.

Many addicts and alcoholics are chronic liars. I was. Not only did I lie about how I was (sober when I was drunk; fine when I was miserable), but I embellished the stories I told about my life. I wanted to be cool, fascinating, extraordinary. For years, I said I had been at the infamous Altamont Rolling Stones concert in 1969 when the truth was I'd been invited to go and had said no. My roommate and three guys she'd picked up in a bar were going, but I was too afraid to go with them. It was a wise choice but not an interesting choice, and so I lied about it. In sobriety, we learn to be with the truth, both the painful and the ordinary, and we tell those stories.

STORYTELLING

Oral storytelling—telling a story, personal or not, in front of an audience—is another creative outlet for stories. This form of performance art is on the increase around the country. There are associations, festivals, even academic degrees in storytelling. My good friend Beth Easter has a Master's degree in storytelling from East Tennessee State University, the national home of storytelling.

Chances are that you are already "started" with storytelling. Most of us told stories as kids, reciting the day's activities to our folks. Later, we often made up elaborate stories to get what we wanted or to support our addiction. My first roommate out of college would make up elaborate stories of family funerals she had to attend every time she needed a few days off. I told enough whoppers in my active drinking days to become a chronic liar.

In recovery, I was introduced to a different purpose for story when I started attending 12-Step meetings. In this form of story-telling, we don't write our stories down and read them, as a memoir writer might do. Instead we generate a version of our story, perhaps to fit into an idea in the reading, perhaps to shed an insight we've just had about the experience that relates to the chairperson's share. At the best of times, we share from the heart.

Story-telling is a similar kind of performance art. There's an audience to listen to you. And the stories told at storytelling concerts are not memorized like lines in a play. Rather they are so well known by the teller that they can be generated. Because of that, no two performances of a story by one storyteller are the same.

Because storytelling is a performance art, extroverts may be more naturally drawn to this craft, but it is also a great experience for us introverts as it is a wonderful way to connect with others in a structured environment.

Getting started with storytelling

Unlike poetry writing, which in the beginning may be best done alone, storytelling is best learned and practiced with others.

- Attend some storytelling concerts in your area. Performances of local groups are often free or very inexpensive. See if this idea appeals to you.
- Consider what kinds of stories you'd like to tell. Folk tales, perhaps from your family's cultural or ethnic traditions? Local history? Biography? Funny stories from your family? More serious stories from your past? You might want to visit the local public or university library and ask a librarian to help you with some ideas and some resources.
- You don't need a large repertoire of stories. You really only need one to get going.
- Join a local storytelling group, where people practice together and support each other in developing their stories.
- There are local, state, and national storytelling networks and associations. Membership will bring access to articles and instructional videos.
- Some people find community classes in improvisational theater helpful for their storytelling craft. Check with local theater companies to see which actors or groups are offering improv.
- Shy about speaking in public? Visit a local Toastmasters club and consider joining one of their inexpensive programs where other people nervous about public-speaking help each other feel more comfortable.
- You may find it easiest to speak to children. Contact your local public library and find out about story hours and how you can get involved.
- You may want to become part of a 12-Step speaking circuit and do your storytelling that way. Check with your local central office.

A Storyteller's Story

Alcoholism runs in my family—two brothers, a sister, an aunt, an uncle. But it didn't touch me until after I left a job in Tennessee and started graduate school. That's when it all fell apart. I couldn't compete with the superior students around me. I hired a tutor and battled my way to a B average. That summer I suffered a grand mal seizure that was diagnosed as epilepsy. I knew otherwise—I knew I was stressed and scared of failure. I finished my degree and moved in with friends in Portland. Through it all, I drank.

I didn't drink for long compared to others, but for more than a decade, I drank several nights a week, shades drawn, waiting for alcohol to deaden the fear. It never did. I finally told my therapist about my drinking. She told me where the nearest meeting was. I poured the last of the wine down the drain and went to a meeting. Even as I hid in the back of the room, I heard stories similar to mine. Soon I moved into the circle and sat with others.

A year later I took my first story-telling and writing workshop. I talked about Hobart, from Bumpass Cove, Tennessee—how this so called "hillbilly" had stopped chemicals from contaminating his community. As I told his story, I realized how he and other mentors in my life had reminded me to speak the truth. I joined a writing and storytelling group and began to craft my creative life.

To quote my good friend, J. P. Reynolds, "Story called forth story." I slowly realized that I was not alone. I began to see myself as never before. And in the seeing, I found my voice, my confidence. None of this would have been possible until I stopped drinking and joined the program.

The fellowship is a safe place for me to share my joys and fears. Thanks to 20 years of sobriety, I self-published my first poetry chap book, *Lineage*, and continue to tell stories with the Portland Storytellers Guild. As a result of sobriety, I am open to the stories around me and have found my creative self.

—Maura Doherty, Portland, Oregon, poet, writer, storyteller. *Lineage* is
available at <u>mauradoherty7@gmail.com</u>

WRITING FICTION

Writing fiction is another way for some of us to process our experiences and the questions we often hold about why we and others have made the choices that we make. Writing fiction is, for some of us, more than telling made-up stories. It's a way to work through more of our questions about life. The novel I'm working on now is the story of what happens to two women when their mother doesn't love them and, in fact, can't. I had a difficult relationship with my mother and while the woman in the novel is not my mother, I am getting a chance to see this experience from both sides.

I started writing fiction by writing prompts. I then wrote some short stories, but I wasn't satisfied by them. And in my paid work, I was editing novels for writer clients. So I decided to write a novel. And why not? I didn't write with any thought of publishing that novel. I didn't write with hopes of becoming rich or famous. I just wanted to know two things: What did it take to write a novel and could I do it? I think that when our creative goal is personal satisfaction, upping the ante by taking on a big project can be an exciting experience.

My friend Jeanine started out doing memoir of her experiences as a drug addict and then felt more comfortable with fictionalizing the characters, including herself. Her novel is called *Shadows and Veins*.

A Novelist's Story

I originally intended to write my story, fact by fact. There were so many intense images, fragments of conversations and memories that I absolutely had to get out of my brain and onto paper. Once I did that and completed the first draft of my book, I found that my relationship to my past had changed. My addiction was no longer sitting on my shoulder, informing my world view; writing it all down gave me distance, space, a view from recovery. I was then able to go back in, again and again and again, to edit and rewrite and shape a fictional telling out of the framework of my life.

In the process of writing *Shadows and Veins*, it came to me that I didn't have the right to tell anyone's story other than my own. Some people, close and otherwise, from my "real" story have gone on with their lives and there seemed no reason to expose what was, for them, a small piece of their distant past. And, I found that writing fiction gave me more leeway to create interesting characters and situations, drawn from my experience but not exclusive to it.

—Jeanine Bassett (shadowsandveins@gmail.com)

Getting started writing fiction

Most writers find workshops, classes, retreats, and groups helpful as they begin writing fiction. Writing can be a lonely business (we each have to do our own) and finding ways to get support and be in community can be really nice. Here are some tips on beginning to find your way into the fiction writing world.

- Read, read, read. If you're interested in writing short stories, read short stories. Read the famous and the new writers. If you're interested in genre fiction, like romance or mystery or young adult, read those. I suggest also that when you find a story or novel that you really admire, read it twice. Read it once for the story and the enjoyment, then reread it to see how the author did it. Read it for language, construction, theme, technique. You'll learn a lot.

- You may want to read some books on writing fiction. One of the most important, I think, is Robert McKee's book *Story*. McKee is a veteran script doctor for Hollywood and he has put together a great book on how to tell a great story, whether you're writing fiction or a screenplay. But after you're read three or four books on the craft, let them go. Reading about writing is not the same as writing.

- Develop a daily writing practice. You might start with journaling or prompts but get in the habit of writing every day. Once that healthy habit is solidly in place, writing a novel or a collection of short stories won't seem so daunting.

- **Writing classes:** Nearly every university, college, and community college offers writing classes, both for regularly enrolled students and for community members. Costs vary with tuition and fees, but most community colleges offer very affordable classes and often have great teachers. For some of us, this kind of structure with deadlines and feedback is a great place to begin or get additional training.

- **Writing workshops and seminars:** Workshops usually occur over a weekend or a week. They are an intense form of a class and offer opportunities to write and read your work to others, sometimes with critical feedback and suggestions. They are often taught by a published writer (part of the way writers make a living) and may be sponsored by a local writers association. Most workshop teachers will be happy to give you the names of former students as references if you want to check them out before you sign up.

- **Writing retreats:** Writing retreats are often a workshop in a vacation setting. You go to a retreat center or a house somewhere, spend time in class with the teacher part of the day, and have lots of writing time on your own. Cost depends on how far you travel, room and board, and teacher's fees. Some writing groups arrange their own low-cost retreats, renting a house at the beach or in the mountains, sharing cooking. Twice a year, I arrange a retreat with writer friends on Whidbey Island north of Seattle where we write in silence all day and then have dinner together and fun evenings. I also offer quarterly mini-retreats (Friday-Sunday) at my home for 3-4 writers.

- **Writing groups:** Writing groups have been around for centuries, people getting together to read their writing and offer support and comments. Many writing groups today are formal critique groups. Members distribute pages of their writing beforehand, the group reads the writing, and then the group advises the writer on how to improve the writing. If the group is kind and the members are not competitive with each other, this can be very helpful. However, a writing support group where there is no formal critique, only listening and encouragement, is often better for beginners.

DRAWING AND PAINTING

Drawing and painting may seem like daunting creative media to take on. After all, they are forms of expression we may most associate with professional artists. But they too have a simple side, an easy-to-approach side. If you've ever doodled, you've drawn. Pen or pencil to paper and no words. That's what drawing is. Painting too in its simplest form is coloring without the coloring book.

Here's where I think most of us get hung up. We can't draw or paint *realistically* with ease. We can't pick up a brush or a pencil and create a photographic portrait or an exact representation of an object or landscape in 20 minutes. For way too long, I thought that that was what artistic talent was: the ability to reproduce reality and do it fast. Now I know that's only one of many kinds of talent and ability. In fact, for most viewers, realistic representation is the least interesting kind of painting because it's the least emotional.

One of the most important aspects of recovery is owning and acknowledging our feelings. I learned early on in my family that the darker emotions of anger and sadness were to be kept to myself. By the time I became an adult, the only way I could let those feelings out was to get drunk. Then the lid would come off the pressure cooker and I could rage at my lover for his infidelities or weep at my disappointments and losses. When I got sober, I had to find another way to release that pressure and express my feelings. Both poetry and painting have been outlets for that expression.

Writing poems lets me find words for my feelings, lets me get them out onto paper. I can be as crude and as angry and as cutting as I need to be. No one reads them but me, no one gets hurt, and I get relief. Painting and drawing abstracts lets me express those emotions for which I have no words. Pushing dark paint around, drawing menacing monsters or gloomy cloud shapes relieves some of that pressure.

Abstract painting is a wonderful place for many of us to start. While it can be highly sophisticated and nuanced, like all the arts, it can also just be pushing paint around into shapes *we* like with colors *we* like. It doesn't have to look like anything—and it probably can't. What does our pain look like? Only we know.

Drawing

As I said earlier, pushing pen or pencil around on paper into shapes is drawing. Wait, you may be saying, it isn't that easy. Well, yes and no. Often when we draw, we intend to draw something. We did that as kids. We drew our families or our house or the house we wish we lived in. We drew horses or motorcycles or unicorns, the things that intrigued us or that we longed for. So in one sense, drawing is *rendering* something or some idea on paper.

But abstraction in drawing also works too. An old friend of mine gets a kick out of doodling with a thick-tipped black pen on a thick white paper. Then she uses markers to color in the shapes and patterns she finds in the doodling. These drawings are very cool. My own play in the studio involves both drawing and painting. I've been working lately on flowers as I love their shapes. So I draw the shapes and patterns I see in the flowers onto my paper in faint colored pencil, and then I color them (I'm putting all that coloring book practice to good use).

And of course you can draw and paint realistically, rendering some object or person that you see onto the paper or canvas. Remember the point of this work is not to make a photograph with a pencil or brush, but to interpret the object in your own way, however that might look.

You can draw with anything that will make marks: pencils, pens, brushes, markers, a knife into a picnic table, a stick in the sand or the dirt. You don't need any special tools and at the same time, art and craft stores are full of special tools. It can be a great joy to experiment and find the ones that have the right feel for you. Similarly, you can draw on anything that will take marks: paper, canvas, cardboard, clay, wood, glass, metal. But most of us start out with paper. Again there are lots of kinds and colors and thicknesses, and I encourage you to explore until you find the surface and the tool that work just right for you. There are sketch pads and drawing notebooks of all sizes. My drawing teacher Phil suggested we get a stack of 4x6 blank note cards and draw something on one every day. Or you can get a small notebook and carry it with you and draw while you're stuck in traffic or waiting in line at the bank or riding the bus.

Getting started with drawing from life

—Bridget

Drawing from life is challenging in part because we think that what we draw should look exactly like what we think we're seeing. We have clear expectations of what the finished image should look like before we even get started. After all, we already have a clear idea of what a cup or a tree or a pencil is supposed to look like, right? Drawing can be a lot more fun if you consider drawing to be a record of your exploration of an object rather than a reproduction of the object.

- Begin with blank paper and a soft pencil (#2 is fine). Forget the eraser for now.
- Choose an object to draw. Start with something simple, familiar, and stationary like a cup or a flower. Save animals, people, and landscapes for later.
- Use your eyes to trace the object. Begin drawing, almost like you're letting your eyes pull your hand in the right direction. Don't be afraid of drawing multiple lines on top of each other.
- Spend more time looking at the object than at the drawing.
- Try to record areas of shadow and light as well as edges.
- Only use the eraser to bring back areas of light that have gotten too dark or to sharpen edges; DON'T use the eraser to erase lines that you think are "wrong." Those lines are just extra observations.
- Keep drawing, adding marks, textures, observations. Add marks that reflect how you feel about the object.
- Stop when you feel like you've recorded everything you have felt and observed in the object.

Getting started with drawing from a photograph

—Bridget

Drawing is all about learning to see. This is a great way to step away from what we think we're seeing and learn to really observe.

- Choose your photograph. It can be a page from a magazine or a favorite snapshot, though a simple image with high contrast or dark lines will work best. Next, make a black-and-white photocopy and enlarge the image so that it's at least 8.5"x11", the size of a regular sheet of printer paper.
- You'll need a pencil, a ruler or a straight-edge, and a piece of paper that's also at least 8.5"x11".
- Begin by creating a grid on the photocopy of your image:
  - Fold the photocopy in half the long way; then fold it in half again. Unfold the photocopy.
  - Fold the photocopy in half the short way; then fold it in half again. When you unfold the photocopy, you should have 16 equally sized rectangles on the paper.
- Use your straight-edge to trace over the lines made by the folds.
- Next, fold your drawing paper the same way. Again, use your straight-edge and a pencil to trace over the lines.
- You're ready to draw! Place your photocopy, or reference image, somewhere where you can easily see it and then turn it upside down. That's right! Upside down.
- Use the grid as a reference, and just draw what you see in each rectangle of the photocopy in the corresponding rectangle of your drawing paper.
- Shade in dark areas and light areas; look closely at shapes and lines and see where they fall in the rectangle and how they relate to the other rectangles nearby.
- By focusing on one shape, one rectangle at a time instead of trying to capture the whole image, you'll teach yourself how to observe more deeply! And you'll be surprised by how realistic the image is.

Getting started with cartooning

—Bridget

Cartooning is about using basic shapes and the fewest possible lines to convey an idea. We forget sometimes that drawings don't have to be hyper-realistic to be recognizable or to communicate an idea. A square with a triangle on top? We all know that's a house or an arrow. A few extra lines or a bit of context, and it becomes clear.

- Think of an object you use every day.
- With a pen (not pencil) and paper and without looking at the object, attempt to draw it. Ask yourself:
  - What are the biggest, most dominant shapes and lines that make up the object? Circle, square, oval, rectangle, triangle, pear shape?
  - What are the things that are the strongest visual cues as to the identity of the object? A squiggle, a texture, a clue to context? Can I exaggerate those cues, make them more obvious?
  - How can I simplify the shapes and visual cues into the fewest marks?
- Try drawing the object several times—try to get it down to the essence.
- Now, draw the object with it in front of you. Again, ask yourself:
  - What are the biggest, most dominant shapes and lines that make up the object?
  - What are the things that the strongest visual cues as to the identity of the object?
  - How can I simplify them?
- By the time you've drawn the object several times both from your memory and from life, you will probably have discovered an easy shorthand that communicates the essence of the object.

Painting

Painting may seem like a daunting art form. We're used to seeing paintings in museums and galleries made by famous artists at the top of their game. And while like with all art forms, there are people who are professionals at doing it, there are also millions of people like me who are amateurs. The word *amateur* comes from the French and means "lover." I am a lover of painting, both as a doer of it and an observer of it. Mostly I just love color, and painting (i.e., pushing color around on paper or canvas) gives me great pleasure and satisfaction.

In some ways, I love painting precisely because I am an amateur. That takes all the pressure off for me. I can have a good time and make crap sometimes and good things other times and it's all okay. It's play for me, not serious business. And I can think this is a key to finding a good creative medium for us—one that encourages us to be playful and light-hearted.

Getting started with painting

- While you can spend a fortune on art supplies, there's no need to. I started off with inexpensive tempera paints from my local super-grocery store's craft section. Tempera paints clean up with water and don't require fancy brushes. They're also best painted on paper so getting a pad of somewhat thick white paper and a couple of cheap brushes (one big, one little) was all I needed.
- A table easel can be handy to have but it's just as easy to paint flat on the kitchen table or kitchen counter. A friend of mine tapes her paper onto her refrigerator and paints there.
- You can also invest about the same small amount of money in an acrylic painting starter kit, which will come with several brushes and 6-8 tubes of color. Acrylic paints are also water-based and clean up with soap and water. They have brighter colors than tempura, you can easily mix new colors from the ones you have, and you can paint over them when they are dry. Acrylics do fine on thick paper and also on canvas (canvas comes in many forms—I use canvas that comes in pads of 12 sheets for convenience as the sheets are already primed). One word of caution: tempura will come out of your clothes but acrylic paint will not.

- Or you can paint with pastels, like I do. Pastels come in two forms (dry/soft and oil). Pastels are basically pigment (color) dust pressed into sticks, with and without oil. If you've ever written on a blackboard or a sidewalk with chalk, you've used a soft pastel. I love them for their color and I find the sticks easier to work with than a paint brush. But that's just my preference. (Soft pastels wash easily out of your clothes.)
- I found it helpful to paint on my own for a while and then take some classes. The instructions meant more to me when I already knew a little of what I was doing. But you might find it easier to start with a class. Just be sure you have a really encouraging teacher. Nothing can shut us down faster in the beginning than criticism, even when it is meant to be helpful.

A word about showing up.

Integrity is not only about telling the truth. It's also about keeping our word. When we were active in our addiction, keeping our word with ourselves or anyone else wasn't a high priority. We often didn't show up for appointments, called with a phony excuse at the last minute, were "sick" a lot for work, didn't pay bills on time. In recovery, we begin to pay attention. We notice our self-talk, we consider what we agree to, and we do what we say we will. It's one of the best ways to make amends to family and friends, by showing up when we agree to.

Artmaking gives us a great opportunity to practice that form of integrity. If we commit to a journaling practice or a poem-a-day challenge or drawing on 100 note cards, we do it. No excuses. If we commit to a creative date to write or paint with friends, we show up. If we tell ourselves we want to try watercolors, we get the materials and we start playing with them. Just as with going to meetings, talking to our sponsors, or doing prayer and meditation, we keep our commitments as we know that's a way to strengthen our recovery.

PROCESS PAINTING

Process painting is a form of creative self-expression rather than a painting technique. It is aimed at allowing the painter to process and express emotions from deep within. I participated in a weekend-long experience with a wonderful Portland teacher, Carolyn Winkler. We were asked to set an intention to be open to the process and to ask a silent question of significance to us. Then we started to paint. We could add paper to our original big sheet but we couldn't start over. We just kept painting and painting and painting on the same painting. We worked in silence next to each other (there were half a dozen of us), and Carolyn would occasionally ask us a question that would send us deeper inside. We never commented on our paintings or on someone else's although we talked about the process on our breaks and at lunch.

I was used to painting from something: a picture, an object, someone else's painting. So this imaginative work terrified me at first. I had only myself to rely on, but eventually I just stopped worrying about making something recognizable and just kept painting whatever came up for me. Over the course of the two days, all my emotions came into play. I was exhilarated, bored, angry, frustrated, tender, contented, peaceful—you name it. And although I hadn't thought of it until just this minute, this workshop was the beginning of all my deeper and sustained writing efforts.

Getting started with process painting

—Bridget

Sometimes, with drawing, we can get caught up with making the imagery recognizable. Painting lets us explore other forms of visual expression—in part, because it's harder to control the shapes that are made with a brush and paint, at least at first. Process painting is a great opportunity to paint purely from the imagination, from the heart, for self-expression and self-exploration. It can place you fully in the moment.

- To start, all you'll need are tempera paints (these work better than watercolors for process painting, and are usually less expensive than acrylics), a small brush, a larger brush, and large paper (I'd recommend 18"x24" paper). You'll also want a dish for water to clean your brushes (I use an old yogurt tub) and a few rags for clean-up.

- Open the colors and ensure that they're well mixed. If you have large containers of paint, you may just want to squeeze a bit of a few colors onto a palette—a plastic plate or a piece of wax paper wrapped around a scrap of cardboard will work just fine.
- Dip your brush in water, dab the excess off on the rag, and dip the brush into the color that most excites you, that calls to you.
- Apply the paint to the paper in a shape that feels good.
- Repeat.
- You may feel drawn to create images, or just to make shapes, or to make dots, or to fill in the paper with color. All of these are just fine. If you get stuck, ask yourself these questions:
  - What have I wanted to paint that I haven't painted?
  - What am I afraid of doing?
  - What would ruin the painting?
  - What's the worst, most horrible, most ugly thing I could do?
  - What do I think I can't paint?
  - What does there need to be more of?
  - Is there anything else that I need to do in the painting?
- If you have a strong reaction to any of the questions or if something pops into your head in an immediate response, try doing it! The idea is to be in the process, not to make some kind of "perfect" image.
- When you think you're done, ask yourself the questions again.
- Keep going until nothing further comes up.

A word about symbols.

Some forms of poetry and painting rely on symbols as part of their meaning. You may think this is complicated or over your head, but we use symbols in daily life all the time. The heart is a symbol for love, the $ is a symbol for cost, a row of tiny chili peppers on a menu means extra spicy. A wedding ring is heavy with symbolic meaning: love, fidelity, commitment. So we all already know about symbols. As you begin to write poems or paint, you might begin to look for your own symbolic language. What represents anger for you? What represents freedom? What represents recovery? And then use those symbols in your creative self-expression.

CREATIVITY AND THE 12 STEPS: INTEGRITY

Admitting the exact nature of our wrongs

When I think of integrity in personal terms, it often means following through on commitments. When I think about integrity in my artmaking, my mind immediately goes to the stacks of UFOs in my studio.

In the world of creative making, a UFO is an Un-Finished Object. It's the painting that got started and never finished, the draft of that novel in the bottom drawer. For me, part of having integrity in my art is coming to a place of completion in my work—and that can be tough to do!

Note, though, that I said my work needs to be completed, not finished. *Finished* implies a polished final product; *completed* means coming to a place where we feel done.

A lot of things can bring me to a halt on a piece I've started: I might come to a place in the piece where I don't know what to do next, or I get bored with it, or I feel like I'm not doing it right. And until I can acknowledge that uncertainty, that boredom, that fear, I can't move forward. I'll just keep moving in circles.

I might decide to get help of some kind to reach resolution, or I might decide that the project is just not as interesting as I thought it would be and I let it go. Either way, I need to make a decision. Letting go of a project is better than hiding a tub full of yarn under the bed, pretending that I'm really going to knit everyone in my family a sweater.

—Bridget

Question: How might you define *complete* for your projects? Will it be a look? A feeling? An intuition? In other parts of your life, what does *complete* feel like?

Suggestion: Commit to going through all your projects on a regular basis. Find a way to move forward on the ones that still have energy for you; let go of the ones that feel stagnant. Talking with a friend can help you figure out which is which.

WILLINGNESS

PUTTING YOURSELF OUT THERE

There is probably no more important attribute for both sobriety and creativity than willingness. In my treatment center, it became pretty clear who was going to make it and who wasn't. Those in the group who had been court-mandated or coerced by concerned family members were always talking about the parties they would go to when they got out. They focused on the fun of drinking, not the misery. An old adage comes to mind: You can lead a drunk to treatment, but you can't make him not drink. Those of us with obvious willingness, who listened, who spoke up about what it had been like and what had happened, we had a chance.

So when we add willingness to the picture, willingness to change, willingness to try new things, willingness to step out a little into something different, the odds for long-term sobriety improve dramatically. The sober life is very different from the using life. In the beginning, we may think it's just a matter of not drinking or drugging or eating or shopping or gambling, but recovery isn't that simple, for just not using in the same life as before is a recipe for relapse. If our lives had been wonderful, we wouldn't have wanted to get sober. So the parts of our lives that don't work have to change. And willingness to try new things is key to that change.

All artmaking requires willingness to try new things. Each knitted sock, each poem, each drawing is a new thing. And while creatives work at honing their skills and developing helpful routines that they can count on, they are also deeply immersed in creating, in bringing forth the new.

DANCE

Artmaking can be about movement. From early cave paintings, we know that humans danced. Dancing to drumming is probably as old as we are. Many people find comfort and relief from anxiety in moving their bodies. Add music and you have a party, even if it is a party for one.

Many of us are inhibited about moving our bodies in more than the usual ways (getting up, sitting down, walking). It took lots of alcohol or drugs for us to get loose enough to get on the dance floor. So we may feel corny strutting, swaying, and boogie-ing away. The awkwardness will pass, believe me. Just keep at it. In many ways, it's no different from the newness and awkwardness of painting or writing poems. We get better with practice. My teacher Phil talks about toddlers learning to walk. They fall down a lot. And it doesn't stop them. They just get up and try again. Their apprenticeship continues. We can turn that same willingness and determination to our creative self-expression.

Dancing can involve public performance, of course. That public can be an informal one. You can go out to a club and dance to music. Or it can be a formal one where you join a group that gives dance concerts or even solo performances. However, both of these may prove problematic to those of us in recovery. Clubs can be dangerous places. They generally serve alcohol and are often a venue for drug sales and use. When we get sober, we often have to give up those old playgrounds, at least for a good while. And the spotlight of a performance can be harrowing for many of us in early recovery. But there are many other dance possibilities.

Getting started with dance

- You can dance in your living room or backyard. Crank up the music and go for it. Or if you have neighbors who may object, turn up your MP3 player and boogie away.
- There's a wonderful YouTube video (*Where the hell is Matt?*) circulating of a young man who dances everywhere, in offices, in the grocery store, walking down the street listening to his iPod. Give it a try.
- Gabrielle Roth has a video and CD program called *Sweat Your Prayers* based on her theory of five distinct rhythms. It acknowledges the long-standing relationship between movement and prayer through recorded tribal drumming rhythms at five different speeds. You don't need the video

to get started, though it's fascinating to watch the dancers and move along with them. There are no instructions (this isn't an exercise video) and no choreography. That's up to you; that's where your artmaking comes in. Her CDs have the same music as the videos, and on your MP3 player, you can sweat your own prayers or sorrow or anger or celebrate yourself in your living room or out on your lawn. And many larger cities also have regular ecstatic dance groups that meet weekly, often on Sunday mornings. Search *five rhythms* or *ecstatic dance* to find a group near you.

- The Dances of Universal Peace are another form of sacred movement. This international organization has groups in many towns and cities and focuses on traditional sacred dances from all faith traditions. The weekly gatherings are 2-3 hours of dancing in a large circle. Dances are taught as they are danced, and beginners are always welcome. It's lovely and slow, and most of the dances are learnable by anyone.

- Contra dancing is a socializing and dancing event. Dances (most require only a smooth walking step) are taught before they are danced. Dances are done in couples that change every dance or two. Beginners are welcome. One veteran described them as modern-day barn dances where everyone goes to have a good time. A friend of mine found contra dances a safe place to be touched by others (in traditional partner dance position) and to make eye contact, all in a non-sexual way. Caution: contra dancing can be addictive.

- Increasingly, there are traditional dance classes (ballet, tango, modern) for adult beginners. Some include recitals or public performances.

- Many gyms and community centers offer NIA and zumba classes, which are a combination of dance and fitness.

A Dancer's Story

I was one of those recovering people who couldn't remember ever dancing in public unless I was drunk. About one year sober, I began taking movement classes again, dance and yoga. In the beginning, the fact of moving my body with other dancers where no one pointed or laughed at me made me feel better about myself. I felt accepted. I kept going back to the dance because I felt an all-over goodness afterwards, partly because of endorphins I'm sure, but also because I was learning to stick with something, learning about myself, and making sober friends who were interested in my creative ideas.

Just moving my body, increasing my breathing, muscle strength, and ability to sweat helped detox my whole system early on in recovery. Dance also helps me locate and remember that I am a whole body self, a swirl of legs, arms, belly, neck, back, not just a head with a brain that can get caught up in addictive thinking.

It wasn't until nine years sober that I started to make and perform my dance works. I was internally ready by then, pretty okay with feeling awkward, not comparing my work to others, able to trust in a power greater than myself, and able to ask friends to help me by being in the audience and smiling a lot.

In dance, willingness to listen to the small still voice inside of me is crucial. When I'm following deep intuition, the outcome of what I'm working on turns out to be greater than what I can create on my own. Tenacity is a great quality, too. It allows me to do what I know is right for me no matter what, whether holding true to my vision of an art piece or leaving in the middle of an important event if my sober self no longer feels comfortable in my own skin.

I hear music with my body, not just with my ears. I am a kinesthetic person who leads her life from her body-sense, but at the time I chose dance, I didn't know this about myself. I was cut off from my body by addictions. An answer that also makes sense to me is that dance chose me. I get to convey feelings we often do not have words for, and share my deeper experience of living in a way that reaches out to others, to share, to witness, and hopefully to know within themselves.

Dance, whether as a medium for making art or for enjoyment, opens the mind to the power of the body we lost while addicted. Some quotes by famous movers relate as much to recovering the authentic self as they do to making dance. Things like "if you do not dance your dance, who will?" and "There is really only One Dance…" I know being a dance/movement creative has allowed me to recover who I was meant to be, and how I am infinitely connected to others and the greater whole.

—Lillian Gael, dancer and performer, lilygael.com

PERFORMANCE ART

Some of us crave an audience. We were the boisterous drunks in the bar, telling stories, telling jokes, doing sit-down routines. When we embrace sobriety, we lose that audience. Being newly sober can be a restless time, with old habits calling to us for relief. One of the great challenges of recovery is finding a way to channel that energy into new activities, ones that bring that relief without drugs or alcohol or chocolate or video poker. Finding that new audience in recovery can be satisfied by exploring performance art.

Performance art covers a broad range of creative endeavors, from acting to stand-up comedy, from story-telling to street singing, dancing, and acting.

All creative endeavors take a big measure of willingness. We have to be willing to show up to the canvas or the stage, the piano or the acting group. We have to be willing to try new things, maybe to show our work to others. Both staying sober and getting deep into a creative practice require a willingness to be more of who we really are, both to ourselves and to others. And it's so worth it to do so.

Getting started in performance art

- Read the section on Storytelling above.
- If you live in a city, local theater companies will have actors who teach acting classes as part of their livelihood. These classes can be a springboard to auditioning for local plays or can be an activity of their own, in which your audience is your classmates. Either way you get a chance to learn lines, rehearse, get directed, and perform.
- Improv classes are also a great way to learn to perform. There are both acting improv classes and comedy improv classes. In most cities, there are open mike nights for improv at comedy clubs and coffee houses (bars have them too but places that serve alcohol are not safe for many of us). In Portland, Oregon, where I live, the comedy clubs regularly sponsor sober nights where no alcohol is served and there's an open mike. Lots of very funny recovery jokes get told.
- Nearly every American town has a community theater. You can volunteer in all kinds of ways and auditions are usually open to all.
- Sometimes movie-making will come to your town. Being involved in the local theater scene is the way to get involved in the movies, whether it's for a television show or an independent film or a blockbuster.

A word about rejection.

Most artmaking can be shared but some forms of self-expression are more public than others. We can paint landscapes and never try to sell a one. We can write poems and never try to publish a one. But if you choose performance dance or acting as your medium of self-expression, in fact, any medium that requires an audience for completion, you risk rejection. You risk auditioning and not being selected. You risk unflattering reviews or indifferent viewers. The same is true of marketing your painting or ceramics or sculpture.

In early sobriety, our fledgling sober egos are fragile and so we're best to go slowly into the performing arenas, sticking with supportive groups and teachers until we can dip our toe into performing in public. Be easy and gentle with yourself if performance is your calling. Gather support and mentors who can help you know when your art is sufficiently crafted for display and your ego is strong enough to accept whatever response you get.

CREATIVITY AND THE 12 STEPS: WILLINGNESS

Becoming entirely ready to have Spirit help me release my defensive habits

Creative self-expression is all about risk. To make art, I need to be willing to risk failure, to risk looking like a fool. I want people to like me. I want to look good. These are some of my oldest, toughest defensive habits. And yes, those are the same defenses that led me into a lot of addictive behaviors. Every time I sit down to make art, I take the risk that I might make something crappy. Every time I sit down to make art, I get to practice letting go of those defensive habits. For me, the risks I take in creative self-expression are great practice in letting go.

At some point in our exploration of creative self-expression, critique or feedback can be valuable. In the beginning though (and maybe a long beginning), just be willing to make stuff. Ignore the critical voice. Ignore the bristling defenses. Be willing to show up. Be willing to let go. Be willing to make something you may not like.

The truth is, you don't have to like what you make. And you don't have to show your work to anyone. You don't need your defensive habits here. Creative self-expression is a great place to risk failing because as long as you show up and make something, you can't fail. To me, this is what it means to become ready to turn the fears and the failures over to Spirit. I no longer have to make decisions based on those fears and I no longer have to tally the failures. I can let go of those defensive habits that have kept me from being fully myself. I can just make the art and let go.

—**Bridget**

Question: What are your fears about creative self-expression? What do you risk by making art in spite of your fear? How might you increase your willingness?

Suggestion: Before you set out to make art, say to yourself: "As long as I show up and make something, I can't fail."

Humility

WORKING WITH OUR HANDS

Getting sober is a tremendously humbling experience for most of us. For years or decades, we tried to control our drinking or shopping, our drug use or gambling. We swore off hundreds of times, we made promises to ourselves and to others—all to no avail. We may have pretended for a time or even for a long time that we were in control of our using, but the truth is our addiction was in control of us. And getting clean, becoming abstinent, means the final giving up of that illusion of control, for we must admit we are powerless over alcohol or sugar or credit card spending and that our lives are unmanageable.

Later, as we work the 12 Steps, we begin to move into a partnership with the Higher Power, however we understand it, to make additional changes that will strengthen our ability to stay abstinent. We look at patterns of behavior and begin to uncover the defenses we've long held between our egos and our true selves, and we ask for help in dropping those defenses so that we can become stronger, steadier, and of more use to ourselves and others.

Sobriety contains many lessons in humility. Our fierce independence isn't helpful anymore. We work with a sponsor and learn to take suggestions and directions. Our best attempts at salvaging friendships with our drinking buddies or a drinking spouse may fail. We may get divorced. We may become estranged for a short while or a long while from our children or other family members who are slow to believe in our changes. Our old boss may be equally slow to accept the new person we are becoming and that job disappears. Rather than riding roughshod through our lives as before, we learn to become slower, more patient, more humble.

Working with our hands in the soil or the clay, with wood or metal, are artmaking activities that can soothe some of our impatience and support our humility. When we work with these materials, we must work in partnership with them, and we must give over the sense that we are in complete control of what happens.

A word about simplicity and complexity in artmaking.

Most creative arts are multilayered. They can be done simply or at a level of great complexity. This is good news for we can start out small, slow, and simple and then move on to more complexity if and when we're ready. I started out coloring with markers on predesigned posters, moved to more elaborate coloring books with colored pencils, and then took my first drawing class. Elapsed time: 6 years. In early sobriety, I felt a strong urge to play with color but I didn't have a lot of time and energy to devote to it. I was going to one or two meetings a day, working full time, and repairing my health and relationships from 20 years of daily drinking. Coloring was a perfect activity for me. I could do a few minutes at a time, I could leave the book and pencils set up on the dining table or kitchen counter, I didn't need a lot of planning or mental energy to do it. Then when I was ready, I moved into classes and put in energy once a week on something more complex. There was no hurry; my artmaking was happy to wait. On the other side, there is no end to where we can go with our creating if we want. There are a ton of things to learn and try and it just gets more interesting.

GARDENING

You may never have thought about gardening as a form of artmaking. And if you perceive it as only a chore to check off your list (got to mow the lawn, got to get somebody to prune the hedges), it isn't. But working with living things is both thrilling and satisfying for many people, and there is much beauty and creating that can be done.

When we were active in our addictions, we often lived in total disregard for our environment. In sobriety, many of us take great pleasure in having a beautiful place to live. And working with the earth, growing healthy things can be both a symbolic and real experience in changing our lives, for many of us find gardening to be literally grounding and centering for our spirits.

Getting started with gardening

- Depending on your space and ambition, you can start out quite small with one large pot on your patio or balcony or front porch. You can buy already blooming plants from a local nursery or garden store and keep your practice as simple as watering, feeding, and tending them. For some of us in early sobriety, this is enough and a wonderful experience in being responsible for another living thing.
- If you have flower beds available to you, you can fill those with blooming plants or you can grow things from seed.
- Another step towards complexity is to have the soil tested (check the Internet for local testers) and do amendments (adding natural ingredients to the soil to make it healthier and more nutritious for your plants).
- If you have shrubs and small trees, you may want to take a pruning class. Check your local nursery for possibilities.
- If you live in an apartment, you could explore bonsai (miniature) trees and their upkeep. This can be a particularly interesting art form with possibilities in shaping, choosing the best ceramic container, and learning how to feed the trees and keep the soil rich.
- If you have a patio or porch, you might be interested in filling hanging baskets with a variety of blooms and colors.
- Garden design is another level up in complexity. Many nurseries, community colleges, and park districts offer courses, and you can redesign your yard or patio space.
- If you have access to larger garden beds or can rent/lease a space in a community garden, growing and harvesting your own vegetables is a wonderful form of artmaking.

A Gardener's Story

I have always loved to garden but until I got sober, it was pretty wishy-washy. After I went through a divorce, I was able to buy a little house that was all my own to do with what I wanted and I did not have to ask permission on what I could plant. The yard was small, but I turned it into my own little sanctuary. I planted wisteria, irises, willow, hibiscus, and many other types of flowers and shrubs along the fence in back. There were so many of those early days of sobriety that I felt like climbing the walls, so I would work in the yard, planting or pruning. Even weeding helped me keep the beast at bay.

I now live in a larger house with my husband. Again the back of the house is small but there is a water feature and I began to add things a little at a time. I've never learned the names and origins. I just plant what I like.

Two years ago my gardening and love of flowers helped me work through another challenge, I was diagnosed with fibromyalgia. I had struggled with chronic pain for years but I always had periods of relief. This time, though, the pain came and never left. I was knocked to my knees with this diagnosis and pain and really felt as though my life as an active person was over.

A couple of good things have come from all this. I started a women's meeting that meets at my house every week, and I am still able to work in the yard. I can't lift heavy pots, but I have a wonderful husband to help with that. And I can still create. This last summer all the years of planting and developing the back yard came to fruition in a secret garden. I sit on my deck and look at all the beauty before me and I am comforted that all is well, I am still sober, and I can still create and build.

I have looked so long for my passion and there it was, right in front of me. I love to garden!

—Diana Y., Calm Clear Woman of the Heart, Spiritual Healer,
Visionary, Earth Steward, and Minister

JEWELRY-MAKING

Like gardening, making jewelry has many facets (pun intended). You can start out small, making a few costume bracelets as gifts for friends, and stay small, at the hobby level, or you can develop your practice into a business that involves high-end gemstones and national shows.

Getting started with jewelry-making

- Nearly every town in America has a bead shop that offers classes and helpful staff that will show you what you need to know to get started, often for free.
- There are thousands of kinds of beads, from plastic to wood to metal, and the combinations are endless. You can start by stringing some of these combinations quickly or you can spend a lot of time designing with colors and shapes and textures. You can even make your own!
- Beads and tools range widely in price as well so you can enjoy this form of art without a big outlay of cash.
- Bead shops also usually have a workspace available and you can meet other beaders and work in community.
- If you find that jewelry-making is your passion, art schools and community colleges offer courses in working with precious metals and gemstones.
- There are beading magazines and guilds and competitions and shows and even beading cruises!

WOODWORKING, METAL-SMITHING

These hand-work media may seem to be a bit more daunting to embark on. They require an outlay of materials and tools and a work space (garage, basement, studio) and perhaps a steeper learning curve at the beginning. But there's plenty of support around.

Getting started with woodworking and metal-smithing

- Unlike some other art forms, taking a class in woodworking or metal-smithing is a good way to start. You can find out if you love it before you invest a lot of money. Most community colleges and art schools offer classes in making small wood and metal objects.
- *Note from Bridget:* Some communities also have tool libraries where, for a small membership fee, you can borrow tools. Here in Portland, there are also several member-based workshops where people pay rent and then have access to larger, more complex tools and workspace.
- A quick search of the Internet shows a number of free video classes and tutorials on both subjects.
- *Note from Bridget:* Consider beginning your woodwork with whittling or relief wood carving, which requires only blocks of soft wood and a simple hand-held wood carving tool. For metal-smithing, a great deal can be accomplished with a jewelry saw and a bench pin; the book *Jewelry Lab* by Melissa Manley is a great place to begin.
- Master woodworkers and metal smiths also offer classes and take apprentices. These are often men and women working in the traditional ways, sometimes with traditional hand-tools instead of power tools. They are eager to keep the traditions alive through teaching them to others. Finding such a teacher is fairly easy. Go into a craft gallery that shows fine metal art or wood art and ask who made the pieces. Chances are good that the craftsmen and women have business cards. They market their businesses just like everybody else.
- As with all art media, these two have associations, guilds, magazines, conferences, workshops, state and regional and national competitions and events.

POTTERY

Like wood arts and metal arts, doing ceramics can be more complicated than some of the other art media. Working with clay is what I call a "messy" art in that you get dirty doing it and it can create a mess where you do it so it's good to have dedicated space (and clothes). Like gardeners though, potters love the feel of the clay and the satisfaction of making a bowl or a mug or a figure come alive in their hands.

Getting started with clay

- Pottery is best learned from a teacher, whether as a student in a class at a community college, community arts center, or art school (most art schools welcome non-degree students from the public or offer special non-credit classes to the public) or as an apprentice to a professional artist.
- Pottery is either built by hand or on a potter's wheel, then depending on the kind of clay, air-dried and painted, or glazed and baked in a special high-temperature kiln. Both the wheel and the kiln are expensive, so most beginning potters use the shared equipment at the arts center or school until they are very sure this is the medium for them.
- *Note from Bridget:* If you want to begin very simply, you can get Sculpey or other air-dry clays at an art supply store. You can use this material to begin shaping forms on a small scale, experimenting with shapes, textures, and the feel of clay in your hands.
- Hand-building can be done on your kitchen table although the clay must be kept moist until you are finished with the project, and the dust and mud make this a garage or basement project for most folks.
- The Internet offers a wealth of information and demos on many aspects of pottery, for beginners and more experienced creatives alike.
- Depending on where you live, clay may be readily available in the soil in your yard or around town. It can be very satisfying to dig your own.

A word about parallel play and creating with others.

Artmaking is both a solitary and a potentially communal experience. We make our own art but we can make it in the presence of others. That's why workshops can be a great deal of fun, especially if they are truly for beginners. There will be little sense of competition and lots of encouragement from the teacher and the other participants to enjoy ourselves and maybe to stretch and risk a little in our making.

It is well known that 12-Step meetings support our abstinence. At the treatment center I attended in Lynchburg, VA, in 1989, a meeting came to the center every night. My first meeting was four hours after I was admitted. I was still drunk, in a daze, full of fear, and yet I experienced something electrical, some kind of energy passing between the many sober folks in the room, something I have felt at almost every meeting since then. I don't know what it is, maybe acceptance, maybe peace, maybe love, but that sharing with others in circle has been a huge support for my sobriety.

There is also an amazing synergy that happens when people create together in the same physical area. It's as if we are all contributing our imagination, courage, and willingness into the common space so that each of us can use what we need or want. When I went to my first writers retreat in 2002, I was struck by the strong sense of being supported. I was writing in my own room during the silent days, but I knew that 14 other writers were equally at work (or play) in their rooms in the three buildings at the retreat center. At meals, we would talk about writing and other art endeavors and our own experiences. Not only did a temporary community spring up, but we wanted the best for each other's artmaking and we put that out into the small world of the retreat and the larger world as well.

When I came back from that first writing retreat, I began to develop ways to get the same support. I signed up for another retreat with the same teacher, and I began to look for other retreats. I didn't find any I could afford so I made up my own, inviting other writers to join me on Fridays for a day of silence and writing on our own projects together. In the last six years, Writing Friday has become a mini-institution. I also organize retreats at a house at the beach twice a year.

CREATIVITY AND THE 12 STEPS: HUMILITY

Asking Spirit to remove my defenses

When I first starting taking classes with Stewart Cubley, I was surprised by one of his standard workshop guidelines: he invited us not to comment on each other's work, nothing, not one word, nada! At that time, I had become used to people who didn't think of themselves as artists complimenting me on my work and people who did think of themselves as artists criticizing my work. Whatever I heard, I swallowed whole. Those comments, positive or negative, replaced my own thoughts and they defined me. So in Stewart's workshop, to make art in the presence of others and hear no comments either way was both terrifying and freeing. It meant that there was only room for me and Spirit in my working process. There wasn't room for *good* or *bad*. All I could do was pick up the brush and apply the paint. I showed up and did the work, letting go of both my fear of judgment and my hunger for praise. Doing the work was enough.

This Step, asking Spirit to remove my defenses, has always been a difficult one for me. I simply cannot accept that Spirit will magically remove my defenses. And yet, the grace that has been offered to me is undeniable. The more I invite Spirit into my life, the more my actions are in alignment with a greater good rather than my own selfish desires. The defensive habits are still there. I'm still my own imperfect self. It's just that those old habits and fears have less of an impact on my decisions and my actions. I'm doing the work, making new habits.

Doing *bad* art doesn't mean we're bad; doing *great* art doesn't mean we're great. It simply means we showed up and made some art. And this is the essence of humility: to show up and do the work without anticipating punishment or reward. The getting-better part will take care of itself.   **—Bridget**

Question: What might help you let go of fear of judgment or hunger for praise and just show up and make something?

Suggestion: Make a sign saying "If I show up and make something, I have already been a success" and hang it up where you do your creating.

LOVE FOR OTHERS

WE CAN'T KEEP IT UNLESS WE GIVE IT AWAY

In the beginning, most of us make art for ourselves. It is our own self that needs soothing, that needs stimulating, that needs pleasing. It is the time on *our* hands that needs to be put to something engaging and satisfying. Just as no one else can get us sober, no one else but us can develop our creative practice. We get sober for ourselves, we get creative for ourselves. But in both cases, those around us benefit from the change in our spirits.

There are also more direct ways in which people can benefit from our creative practices. Some of us choose to make practical art, art objects that serve a functional purpose. Potters may make clay pieces for display or they may make mugs and plates and bowls. Woodworkers may make sculptures or a finely turned box that can hold jewelry or keepsakes. Similarly, fiber artists may make wall hangings or a quilt for a bed or wearable art—socks, caps, clothing of all kinds.

Active addiction is a self-centered thing. I do not say *selfish*, for selfish implies a choosing to think of ourselves first; and once we are addicted to the substance or activity, we no longer have the power of choice. However, our focus is on our relationship with the substance or activity. It becomes, in fact, our primary relationship. While I was a high-functioning alcoholic, my only real concern in the last seven or eight years of my drinking was getting enough: buying enough alcohol, having enough, pretending to not be drunk, getting rid of the bottles. In truth, my full-time occupation was monitoring my behavior and my supply.

In very early recovery, our focus often still remains ourselves. We come into a new relationship with our bodies and health, either feeling much better or dealing with the consequences of our using. We stick close to the program, working with a sponsor, working the Steps, going to meetings. And if we have a spouse or children, we begin to repair those relationships too. But bit by bit, as our health improves and our sanity returns and we grow stronger in sobriety, we begin to branch out into service, into considering the communities in which we live. We may set up chairs for a meeting or make coffee. We may choose to sponsor others in the program so that our recovery community can thrive. Outside of recovery, we may decide to volunteer in one of the myriad programs that help seniors or animals or those in distress.

Similarly, we may choose to make art not just for our own satisfaction but to bring warmth and joy into the lives of others. The fiber arts are a wonderful way to do this.

FIBER ARTS

Working with yarn or cloth may be one of the simplest art forms to begin with, not because they are inherently easier but because many of us have been exposed to them before. If our parents or grandparents or great-grandparents grew up during the Great Depression or WWII, they were most likely very thrifty people who knew how to do many things for themselves. In an era before most people bought ready-to-wear clothing, they knew how to knit and sew. And they may have passed along some of that knowledge to us. My sisters and I learned to knit from our mother, and my sister Kerry taught both of her sons to knit when they were younger. Some of us had home economics classes in school and learned to sew, or we attended 4-H or Scouts and learned some fiber crafts there.

Sewing, knitting, and crocheting can be as simple and straightforward or as complex as you like. Simple patterns are very meditative to work on. They keep our hands busy while letting our minds sift and sort through ideas or reach imaginative solutions for our problems. On the other side, complex patterns are fully engaging and give us a place to focus our attention, thus soothing anxiety.

Getting started with fiber arts: sewing and quilting

Making art with woven cloth is what is known as a *fiber art*. Most of us have done some simple sewing: mending a hem, putting a button back on, shortening a pair of pants or a set of curtains. Or more ambitiously, you may have made your own clothing and have a sewing machine stashed in a back closet or the basement. Wearable art has become high fashion. And quilting, both for wall hangings and as bed coverings, is a long-standing tradition with both standard patterns of design and the possibility of creating any design and combination of fabrics you choose. Quilts can be made with hand-stitching, machine-stitching, or a combination.

- While I haven't touched a sewing machine since I made a pair of badly hemmed curtains for my bedroom in Berkeley in 1969, friends tell me the new digital machines are amazingly easy to use and offer a wealth of stitches and techniques. If sewing again or for the first time intrigues you, you might ask around to see who has a machine you could try out before you make the investment. When you're ready to take the plunge for your own machine, craigslist and other online venues often list both used and new machines.
- Many cities have sewing studios where quilting, wearable art, and basic sewing classes are held. The studios are often a dealer for the new digital machines. Art schools and community colleges also offer classes in sewing, quilting, and tailoring/altering.
- Apprenticing to an art quilter is another possibility. You would spend time in her studio helping out and learning the skills you need in design and execution. You might also consider teaming up with a painter who would create the designs in paint and you could execute them in cloth.

A Fiber Artist's Story

I was in college when I realized I had a problem.

Of course, the addictive behaviors had been there all along, born out of my own innate sense that I was not enough and, at the same time, too much. I was too much emotion, passion, impulse, anxiety, hunger, loneliness, desire, need. There was never enough of anything to fill those gaping holes. And I simply did not believe that I was enough of anything else to be loveable.

As a kid, I had made things, built things, drawn things without feeling that kind of pressure. I got my first sewing machine when I was 5, madly piecing awkward doll quilts from my mom's fabric scraps. I was an only child, anxious and emotional, but I could keep myself happy for hours creating elaborate costumes, environments, and stories for me and my stuffed critters. I even made my own "magazines" with scrap paper, a stapler, and some rubber stamps. I was creating my own world. All of this got me labeled as an artist early on, but in our culture, the word *artist* has a lot of baggage. As I got older, I started feeling like I could never live up to all the things I thought being a "good" artist meant.

In my early years of recovery, art was just one more thing I used to make myself loveable in other people's eyes. Still, there I was at a liberal arts college, majoring in studio art, because I knew deep down that I loved making things more than anything else in the world.

My college included painting, drawing, sculpture and printmaking in the fine arts department. Things like weaving, jewelry-making, fiber arts, pottery, and photography, though, were rarely classes for credit. We had instructors in all of those things, but they were non-credit classes that we students took for fun. The work rooms were in the basement of the student center, not in the art building.

The year I stopped drinking, I started spending a lot more time in that basement because there I could make things without worrying about a critique or a grade. The art I did for class was one thing; this, this I got to do it just because I loved it. I tried weaving, dying fabrics, making jewelry. The instructors all knew me, and eventually, I got a key and 24-hour access. Any time I felt anxious or alone, I could go there. In that basement, I had a refuge.

After trying a lot of things, I settled into batik, a method for dying fabric that uses wax to make patterns. Like most art forms I love, batik involves building up layers: layers of wax, layers of colored dyes, and even layers of different fabrics. There are also a lot of sequential steps in batik: once I started a project, I could walk into the studio knowing what I needed to do next.

Part of the attraction was the physicality of batik: creating patterns in wax, mixing vats of dye, crackling waxed fabrics, dipping and wringing and hanging. It gave me an outlet and a focus for my anxiety. And I could afford to do a lot of it. Fabric yardage was cheap, and the dyes and wax were included in my modest studio fees.

Another thing that made batik perfect for me in early recovery was the sheer chaos of it: the process of batik is unpredictable. I learned to enjoy having wax drip or crack in unexpected places or discover that a blue cloth dipped in a green dye wouldn't necessarily come out the deep blue-green I was hoping for. Instead, I might end up with an oddly brownish blue color. But those "mistakes" became backgrounds for a silkscreened image or got pieced into a fabric collage.

It would take me 20 years to realize it, but the thing I got from making all that fabric was the same thing I had gotten from playing with fabric scraps and a sewing machine on the floor of my room as a kid: I got to be enough.

—Bridget Benton

Getting started with knitting and crocheting

These fiber arts have seen a major comeback in popularity in the last decade, with locally owned stores full of scrumptious colors and textures of yarn and ribbon.

- Yarn stores are usually staffed with very knowledgeable people who can answer all your questions, offer quick lessons and suggestions, and help you choose a project that's right for your current level of skills.
- Many stores offer classes and even more importantly, they often offer a community setting of couches or chairs and tables for group knitting sessions. You bring your project and work on it while others work on theirs. More experienced knitters or crocheters will help you if you get stuck or drop a stitch. Conversations are far-reaching, and it's a great way to meet people with a common interest.
- Thousands of patterns exist for projects: sweaters, coats, caps, gloves, socks, suits, capes, afghans, anything that can be made of yarn. I came across a book recently that had patterns for knitting a small replica of your breed dog!
- As you grow more experienced, you may want to create variations on the patterns or create your own patterns. You may want to learn to spin and dye your own yarn. Fiber association shows and online sellers have all the supplies you need to do that.
- Costs can be low for synthetic yarns. Knitting and crochet needles are also low-cost and last forever. I still have crochet hooks from my teens. Or if you are willing to invest more, handspun and dyed yarns can be quite spendy but gorgeous.
- Although fiber arts are mostly considered a women's world, men are very welcome in most knitting stores, and many more men are taking up knitting for its therapeutic value.

A word about kits and patterns.

Traditionally, a distinction has been made between art and craft, with art seen as more imaginative and craft seen as conforming to set patterns. This cultural distinction has made art superior to craft. However, I think a different distinction is more pertinent. Art is more often decorative and craft is more often functional. Both are of great value to us.

I spoke earlier about the multilayered nature of most art media, and the art/craft division belongs in that conversation. For example, paint-by-number kits, which focus on developing skill rather than developing imagination, are craft under the first distinction. They conform to a set pattern. So does knitting to a simple pattern. Neither outcome is highly original. However, copying the paintings of the old Masters is a time-honored way of learning to paint. So learning one's craft (skills) through kits and patterns is often a first step to becoming more creative.

Just as having a few years of sobriety under our recovery belts makes life easier, so does having a few simple patterns under our creative belts make artmaking easier.

MORE FIBER ARTS

In our homes, everything that is made of thread or yarn was designed and created by someone, and you can become one of them. You can learn to make rugs (hooking, crocheting, loom weaving); you can make pillows and curtains and towels and blankets and kitchen linens and table runners. Or you can make dolls, like one of my sponsors does. Here are a few more artful possibilities.

Needlepoint and embroidery

Needlepoint is a very old fiber tradition of weaving colored yarn into the holes in special canvas. It is a kind of painting with yarn. It comes in kits and patterns, both simple and highly complex. And of course you can create your own designs. Embroidery is embellishing cloth with colored threads in special stitches and knots. Any fabric can be embroidered, from a simple white blouse to a large tablecloth.

Weaving

Another ancient fiber technique, weaving is making cloth of yarn or threads, usually with the aid of a loom. There are handlooms (ever make potholders?), table looms in varying sizes, and large floor looms. Starting small is a good way to go. Weaving takes a certain amount of patience and precision. At the same time, it can be deeply meditative.

Painting on fabric

Most large fabric stores and art stores carry special paints that can be used on fabrics. You can paint on t-shirts, dresses, quilts, furniture, hand towels, sheets, pillow cases—you name it. There are stencils and design transfers that can be used or you can paint freehand. It's inexpensive and fun.

Using fiber in other arts

Cloth, threads, and yarns can be used in other arts. Picasso and his fellow Cubists, who were master collage artists, collaged bits of fabric into their paintings. Fibers are often used in jewelry-making; some are used in ceramics, others in sculpture and mask-making. As always, the possibilities are endless in artmaking.

A Dollmaker's Story

I have always been a tactile person. I had to touch everything and if I didn't like the feel, I didn't have it around me. So it's probably not surprising that fiber art chose me. I dabbled in other media—watercolor, drawing, writing, clay—until I found a way to incorporate many of these media into one. I love fantasy. My favorite stories have always been about elves, fairies, witches in the woods, so now I create whimsical dolls that incorporate clay, painting, sculpting, and a wide range of fibers.

Although I've worked with fabric a long time, I still take a class now and then to keep in touch with other fiber artists and keep the juices flowing for learning new things. When I first got sober, I'd sit in meetings knitting or quilting. It seemed to me that if I kept my hands moving, I could listen better. This is still true. I sit in my weekly women's meeting with my knitting.

It is through my art that I can lose myself and only when I lose myself can I find Spirit. My connection to Spirit is the heart and soul of my recovery. When I'm creating, I go to some place indescribable, the piece is created by my hands; however the essence of it comes through me from Spirit. With my Goddess dolls, my textile art pieces, my hands guide the work and in this way, I connect to a Source much greater than myself and it is this Source that has guided my recovery for the last 30+ years. I would not have the recovery I have today without this connection to Spirit/Source.

I believe the art form chooses us. Whatever form of art a person leans towards needs to be one that speaks to them, one that holds their fascination and imagination. Fabric found me when I was very young and it still holds me close to it.

—Mary M., Vancouver, Washington, doll-maker extraordinaire

A word about balance and time.

Just as spouses sometimes don't understand how often we need to go to meetings to stay sober and be all right within ourselves, they may not always understand our need to paint or make bowls or write on our memoir. It may help that some of these things we can do at home or do with them. But as always, we need to balance our commitment to ourselves and our commitment to others.

CREATIVITY AND THE 12 STEPS: LOVE FOR OTHERS

Becoming conscious of those we have harmed, including ourselves

In 2003, my father died. He was relatively young, his illness sudden, the relationship challenging. There was no real opportunity for closure. That winter, my best friend gave me a painting. The inspiration for the painting was a photograph of my father and me when I was an infant. My dad looks painfully young and happy to be a father; I am smiling, making a grab for his finger, my toes splayed out. The image, as reinterpreted by my friend, brought me to tears.

My friend does almost all of her paintings based on vintage snapshots. This work is what she naturally does as an artist. While this painting was her artwork, a gift spoken in her voice, it wasn't a monologue. She recognized how difficult my father's passing had been for me, and she made something of that experience just for me. She was drawn to the image in part because of the subject but also because, in those splayed toes, she saw the grown woman she knew and loved. Art starts as a monologue but it can turn into a conversation, a way for one person to express her love for another. It need not be elaborate to be a real expression of love. My 4-year-old niece put a pink bead on a purple cord and gave it to me. And it filled me with joy to receive it.

As part of working the Steps, we learn to develop an awareness of when we have harmed another. Through our creativity, we have the opportunity to deepen our understanding of others. When we begin to consider who might benefit from our artmaking or how it might be put to use by others, we begin to incorporate our need for self-expression into the needs of the larger world. We share love instead of harm.

—Bridget

Question: In what ways might you express or share love with your creativity? Who in your life might benefit from an expression of your creativity?

Suggestion: Keep it simple. Your artmaking doesn't have to be elaborate, or even directly shared with the other person, to be an expression of love.

JUSTICE

THE COMMUNICATION ARTS

Doing Step 9 of the 12 Steps involves making amends to those we have harmed. This may mean making a sincere apology, paying back money borrowed or taken, or doing what are called *living amends*. There are often people we have harmed or cheated to whom we cannot make direct amends, so we commit to treating others well in similar circumstances. I was a college professor during my active drinking years and was often drunk or hung-over in the classroom; I wasn't fully present to the students and I wasn't well prepared. While there was no way I could make direct amends to those particular students, I could be a fully present teacher in my classrooms in sobriety.

Step 9 goes beyond apology and repayment. It helps us become responsible in our lives. Active addiction often encourages us to throw responsibility out the window. We become obsessed with alcohol or drugs or gambling or new sex partners, and we lose the ability to care who we hurt, whether it's ourselves, our family, our friends, or our community. In sobriety, we become aware of our actions and take responsibility for them.

How we make amends for our years of not caring is as individual as the items that show up in our inventories in Step 4. But we become attuned to justice and integrity and caring about the welfare of others. Many forms of artmaking lend themselves to direct and indirect efforts for justice and bettering the world. And all forms of artmaking are a wonderful support in learning to be responsible for our feelings and to express them in healthy ways.

In addition, I see artmaking as a positive force in the world. There is an abundance of destructive energy in the universe at this time. I believe that every time we use our creative energy to make something beautiful or interesting or helpful, we right the balance of creative/destructive just a little bit.

Many, many people use their available creativity for less healthy purposes: to influence other people to buy more, to work harder, to vote a certain way. They scheme and plot how to have more power and more money, rather than helping to make the world a better place. I think our world would change dramatically if every politician had an active outlet for creative self-expression, if CEOs were more satisfied by playing the cello or writing a screenplay or painting the view out the window than making a fortune off the mass-production of handguns.

Many of us in recovery are no stranger to violence. We've been beaten or done the beatings. We've been raped or done the raping. We've driven drunk with no thought for the danger to others. We've neglected our families, our pets, our friends. We've been careless with the environment. We have a lot of amends to make. After the personal amends to all those we can reach, we can use creative self-expression as another form of amends to help right the balance in our own lives of destruction and creation.

WRITING FOR JUSTICE

More than many people, alcoholics and addicts know the power of words. We have seen first-hand how our lies and our outspokenness in the wrong moment have hurt people in our lives. We have witnessed the power of apology and confession.

Poetry and its cousin songwriting have long been favorite tools of creatives working for justice, both personal and social/political. Traditional folk songs often have a reforming theme, and the revival of this tradition in the 1960s by singer/songwriters like Joan Baez and Bob Dylan has kept the idea going. Other writing genres like essays and blogs are also good media for sharing information and calling others to action.

Getting started with writing for justice

- If poetry is your creative medium, consider writing a series of poems that inform and move people to action on a cause dear to your heart. Whether it's global warming or saving a row of old trees in your neighborhood, stopping the use of child soldiers around the world or advocating for arts in your local school district, such poems can provide a great outlet for your thoughts and feelings and may prove helpful to organizations who share your concerns if you wish to go public with them.

- Letter-writing may not seem like an art form but it can be. Carefully expressed ideas and suggestions to the editor of local and national newspapers and magazines are a time-honored tradition in the justice movement. And the letter-writing or *epistolary* arts are an equally old tradition. Writing letters for Amnesty International and the American Buddhist practice of letter-writing opportunities to Buddhists in prison are two organized ideas. The 12-Step programs have their own prison and hospital work of taking program meetings in to those who are incarcerated; letter writing your experience, strength, and hope to the members of those meetings could be a fine idea.

- Blogging is, in many ways, a more public form of letter-writing. Blogs are free and easy to set up. They tend to gain a stronger following if the posts center on the same topic. Blogs can be long or short and posted intermittently or regularly, depending on your own needs and inclinations.

- Once we left school, most of us hoped to never write another essay again, seeing them as forms of ritualized torture imposed by the teacher. And no wonder. They weren't about what we thought but instead a regurgitation of what we had learned. Those old school essays bear little resemblance to the creative essays that lie at the heart of good magazine writing and most nonfiction books. Creative essays can easily grow from blog posts, and online is a perfect place to share your thoughts. Reading a lot of well-written essays is a great way to improve your writing and to become familiar with the genre. While essay writing does have basic rules that can be learned from any college textbook on writing, learning from the masters is a lot more fun. Barbara Kingsolver, Terry Tempest Williams, and Wendell Berry, who write primarily on environmental issues, are some of my favorite essayists.

SINGING AND SONGWRITING FOR JUSTICE

Singing is as natural to human beings as breathing, as natural as dancing with our bodies and drawing with a stick in the sand. Artmaking is not some special talent or skill; it's a natural part of our expression of our thoughts and feelings. Sure, some people are naturally good at things: they show an exceptional aptitude very early for throwing a ball or singing on key every time. But that doesn't mean the rest of us can't do it. And I think we all should.

If we all sang and danced and painted our hearts out, I believe the world would be a happier, more peaceful place. Why? Because so much of the world's pain and sorrow comes from bottled-up feelings, resentments, angers, sorrows, guilt. In the program, we say that resentment is a luxury we alcoholics can't afford, not if we are to remain clean and sober. We must express those feelings in meetings, to our sponsor or spiritual director and, I suggest, in our art work.

For artmaking is not just about the pretty and the joyful. It's about all that is dark and unknown in us as well, both our private darkness and our public or collective darkness. Singing our pain, our worries, our outrage has long been an outlet for people. In fact, a whole genre of singing and songs came out of the American South that did just this: the Blues. Our painting, our writing, our singing can absorb that darkness, express it for us, relieve us of its burden. And it doesn't have to be shown to another living soul until we are ready. And maybe not ever.

Getting start with singing and songwriting

It may seem a little silly to give ideas for beginning to sing as we all know how to do it, just like dancing can be done by moving any part of your body. But here are some ideas to help you channel your natural ability to sing into a creative practice.

- In addition to spontaneously singing along with tunes on your MP3 player or the radio, make a conscious effort to sing while you do some regular activity, like doing the dishes or folding the laundry. You might sing about that activity and how much you hate it or how it is a contribution you are making to your family.

- Try singing when you are angry. Stuck in traffic? Sing. Just got cut off by some idiot who made a sudden left-turn without signaling? Sing about it. Cat pooped all over the rug while you were at work? Sing it. If you feel anxious about doing this in the presence of others, do it only when you are alone.

- Try singing when you're angry with someone in their presence. I guarantee it will change the energy, especially if you can get the other person to sing their feelings as well.

- Try singing when you are sad, overwhelmed, or in physical pain. Focusing the breath in this way can be quite meditative and some say healing.

- If you're writing poems about injustice, try singing them aloud when they are completed. Any poet, however inexperienced, can write lyrics. Maybe you play a musical instrument and can set your words to music. Maybe you have little clue about how music works but you can still create a melody and if you want, you can team up with a musician to write that melody down.

- I met a music teacher once and when I told her I couldn't sing, she said that wasn't true. "Even the deaf can be taught to sing," she said. "You just have an untrained voice." If you'd like to train your voice, seek out a local music teacher. You can take private or group lessons, and recitals in public are optional. A friend of mine took music lessons from a wonderfully encouraging man so she could sing a love song to her girlfriend for her birthday. It can be that simple and that private.

- Want to sing with others? Nearly every church has a choir. Nearly every town has a community chorus. Other less formal groups can be organized by anyone. I know a woman who sings in a group called the Tone Rangers that practices old tunes and sings them in nursing homes at the dinner hour. She loves the singing, the group, and the joy they bring to people.

- Take a class in songwriting or poetry with a justice theme. Form a group interested in protesting or advocating through song.

A Songwriter's Story

Long before I was introduced to drugs and alcohol, I was getting high on music. We know that music impacts the same dopamine receptors in the brain as drugs and alcohol, so the connection for me wasn't surprising. As a kid, I listened to the records of my older siblings and felt transported into a fantasy world. Later, I would listen to music when I was drinking and all those good feelings were intensified. And then after I got clean and sober, music seemed a safe way to still get high and feel good.

In my early 20s, a program friend introduced me to traditional country music, and then my job as a newspaper reporter allowed me to interview some famous country stars. I was 22 at the time so this was heady stuff and I felt inspired to learn to play this kind of music myself! In early sobriety I had a lot of time on my hands so in addition to going to meetings and working the Steps, I taught myself to play the guitar.

Then a couple of years into the program, I didn't get a job that I had applied for. The disappointment felt crushing and I needed a way to handle the grief, so I went to my basement and I wrote a song about the experience. It was wonderfully cathartic, a way to work out those intense feelings through creative expression, a way to turn the pain into something beautiful. I later got the job so maybe putting my energy into music instead of fretting helped me release it to the Universe and allowed the job to come to me.

In addition, unlike my newspaper career, writing songs was something that was all mine. I wasn't dependent on anyone else to make it work or have it happen. I made the songs; I created them out of my own brain and experience, and no one could take that away from me. No one can take our creative expression away from us.

—Elisabeth Ames of Elisabeth Ames and the Countrypolitans,
Portland, Oregon

OTHER ARTMAKING SUGGESTIONS FOR JUSTICE WORK

- *The AIDS Quilt Project:* To commemorate the name of someone who has died from the disease, anyone can make a 3'x6' quilt and add it to the larger project. The quilts travel the country and are exhibited in museums, galleries, schools, community centers, and libraries to increase awareness of this deadly disease.

- *Donating a piece of your artwork to a charity or non-profit auction:* Most charities are always looking for fund-raising ideas, and silent and spoken auctions are a popular event. Offering a piece of your work can do two things: bring them some supportive funds and bring joy to the purchaser.

- *Public mural projects:* Near my home is the central office of a musicians union. On the exterior wall of the building is a wonderful mural painted by a number of artists commemorating music styles and the struggle of musicians. Watch for mural-painting opportunities.

- *Create a poetry post in your yard and post poems that raise awareness.* My friend Maura put up a sell-your-house real estate post in her yard, the kind that has a clear plastic box for flyers. She added a second box and labeled one *Take One* and the other *Leave One.* Every week she puts copies of her poems and photos in the Take One box. Within two days, they are all gone. She also finds all kinds of poems, quotes, and drawings in the Leave One box. Her husband Ken, who is a metal smith, embellished the post with some of his artwork.

CREATIVITY AND THE 12 STEPS: JUSTICE

Making amends to those we have harmed

Back when I had my t-shirt business, I made clothes with goddess images on them because I loved the voluptuous forms, the symbolism, the celebration and exploration of the Divine feminine. As I began selling the garments, I offered them in an array of colors and the "usual" range of sizes: S, M, L, XL. In those first few months of selling, I had several women ask me why I was doing images of goddesses but not selling goddess sizes (i.e., sizes over XL). Another friend, who was very petite, commented how hard it was to find "adult" clothes in sizes that would fit her.

These comments blasted my awareness wide open. My mother had struggled with her weight and had been a plus-size woman for most of my teen years, and I had observed first-hand the difference in the way she was treated when she was heavier. I had struggled with body image issues myself and questioned mainstream media's representations of beauty. I realized that this venue, selling hand-decorated clothes to the public, was my chance to raise awareness and do one small thing to heal the way women looked at their own bodies. I found sources for larger and smaller garments, and began making shirts, vests, dresses, and more in sizes XS through 10X.

Making those garments became not only my job but also my activism, my work to right the wrongs of size discrimination. Hundreds of women bought those shirts, some with tears in their eyes at finding a loose-fitting shirt or a positive image of a woman/goddess with their body type. We can, through our own creative expression, raise awareness, heal a wound, right a wrong, and pursue justice.

—**Bridget**

Question: What injustices or wrongs in the world are you sensitive to? Do any of them present topics you might want to write or paint or create about?

Suggestion: Your work can come from a place of love. Angry about deforestation? Try taking pictures of old-growth forests, capturing their beauty, and maybe using those images in your creative work. Find a cause you're passionate about and see what kind of a creative project you could plan.

PERSEVERANCE

ONE DAY AT A TIME

There is only one way to fail at sobriety: stop doing it. Stop going to meetings, stop talking to your sponsor, stop praying and meditating, stop doing the healthy things we've learned how to do. Sooner or later, and mostly sooner, most of us will pick up a drink or a drug, a gallon of ice cream or a deck of cards.

There is also only one way to fail at creative self-expression. Stop doing it. There is no other way to fail at making art. Sure, you can write bad poems or make bad pots or bomb on the stage, but you haven't failed. You've just had a bad episode. Every artist makes crap. Picasso made crap, a great deal of it. That was how he learned.

You don't give up when you hit a bad patch. If you don't keep drawing, my teacher Phil says, those bad drawings (poems, songs, pots) will wait in your arms, so it's best to just get them out. I've found that when I'm consistently painting lousy stuff, if I just keep going, keep turning them out, keep showing up, something new and very interesting is trying to come through.

Remember that like sobriety, artmaking in whatever form is a process, not the products that may (or may not) come from doing the process. And that process occurs one day at a time, one recovery or creative effort at a time.

I hated the idea of one day at a time when I was newly sober. I was still so black-and-white in my thinking that I wanted a guarantee that if I did the 12 Steps, I'd be cured. Of course, I'd wanted that cure for a long time while I was drinking. I wanted something simple that didn't have to be worked at that would just fix whatever was wrong with me. And of course, recovery doesn't work that way. It's not accidental that the program is 12 Steps, not 1. We have to *get* sober. *Get* is a word we commonly use for a process.

Although some of us have had the desire to drink or use or shop or gamble lifted from us, for most of us those desires have to slowly be replaced by other habits. In fact, researchers believe that sobriety occurs as new pathways are created in our brains. The old impulse to use got rewarded many, many times and developed a well-worn path in our brains so that we didn't even think about it. When the impulse hit, we didn't choose, we just used. This concept was helpful for me in understanding why I could remember opening a bottle of wine and remember pouring the last glass but not remember any of the getting up, going to the kitchen, pouring the drinks, or drinking them that went on in-between.

For a long time, my writing was kind of hit or miss. I mostly only wrote when I went away for a weekend or a few days with other writers. I talked about writing a lot in-between but that was all it was, just talk. Then I made a commitment to write each morning, most mornings of the year. I've written a lot more, I've learned a lot more about the craft of writing, but mostly I've just been so much happier. Writing is a meaningful and joyful activity for me, even when I'm stuck, even when it isn't going well. When I write in the morning or when I go to the studio and paint, my whole day goes better. I am more my best self.

All forms of artmaking benefit from perseverance. We keep learning, we keep practicing, we try out new things. We get new ideas and it takes a while to figure out how to do them. We meet new teachers, we take different workshops, we read up on a technique that intrigues us and we work on that for a while. Artmaking is a lifelong process just as recovery is a lifelong process.

Some forms of artmaking don't require a lot of perseverance to produce stuff. Some don't take much training. You can learn to make a very cool collage in a couple of hours. But other art forms just naturally require perseverance, for example, playing a musical instrument or doing large sculptures.

MAKING MUSIC

Many of us took music lessons as kids: piano, drums, violin, a clarinet, or a guitar. This may have lasted a few months or a few years until our interests changed or we realized we were never going be a concert player or a rock star. While you may be beyond rusty, the skills you learned before are still in your body and memory and they can be dusted off.

Getting started (or restarted) making music

- Music stores rent, lease, and sell instruments. It's easy to find something that will fit your budget. They also usually have a good line on teachers who specialize in working with adult beginners.
- Some instruments now come in digital versions so you can practice with headphones. Only you hear the music, saving the neighbors and members of your household the discomfort of those early efforts.
- While the road to a professional life as a musician is long and hard, and may not be advisable for those of us in recovery (bars and taverns are a common venue for musicians to play), there are as many informal opportunities to play and practice with others as you want to organize.

A word about creating something every day.

Our sobriety is usually strongest if we attend to it every day. We learn early on to incorporate prayer and meditation, readings from the literature, meetings, and contact with our sponsor into our day. In this way, we cultivate sobriety. In a sense, we become "good at" sobriety.

The same is true of our artmaking practice. The more regularly and frequently we do it, the more solidly it becomes a healthy part of our lives, a solace when we are down or disturbed, a habit of turning towards engagement, peace, and freedom. And doing a lot of art, whatever our medium, is the only way to get good at it. And for most of us, the better we are at the skills involved, the more satisfying our time is while we're doing it.

It is best if we attend to our art practice every day. As I mentioned, I write for 30-45 minutes every morning when I first get up. In the winter, I sit, as I am this morning, with candles lit in my small sacred space. Sometimes the words flow easily, other times they do not and I have to wait. But I stay off the Internet and in my seat and eventually I solve the issue at hand or know what's next and I write something.

In the same way, I've learned to do something, some little thing, every day with my painting practice. I do my best to get to the studio 3-4 days a week. I usually spend an hour and a half or two hours there painting. On the days I don't go to the studio, I spend a few minutes looking at an art book or making a quick sketch. I can always find 5 minutes to do something. You can too.

SCULPTURE

Sculptures are 2-dimensional and 3-dimensional representations of reality or abstractions. A house built out of playing cards is a sculpture. So is a sand castle. So is an finely honed figure of stone or bronze by Auguste Rodin. The knit-your-own dog book mentioned above has patterns for 6" sculptures of your family pet. Sculptures are made of wood, stone, clay, cloth, yarn, paper, even trash. Here again the possibilities are endless.

Sculpting can be intuitive or planned. Some sculptors begin by gathering materials and then seeing what they can make. Others have a loose or exact idea (perhaps with some preliminary sketches) before they begin. While there are very simple and elegant sculptures, many of these kinds of projects take both well-honed skills and a long time to create. But the efforts can be well worth it in satisfaction and it's a great way to practice patience and perseverance.

If you've visited galleries or museums, you will be familiar with bronze sculptures. These permanent sculptures may seem daunting. And they are. These are the products of an elaborate process that is expensive and not usually undertaken until the sculptor is quite experienced. But sculpting can happen on a much simpler scale. Most people begin with small clay figures and objects to hone their skills. These can be fashioned by hand and air-dried, oven-dried, or baked in a kiln and painted. Clay sculptures can be a long process and you need to have somewhere to work where the pieces can be left undisturbed between sessions.

Getting started with sculpting

- You can begin with hand-building sculptures of various kinds of modeling clay, like Sculpey and Fimo. Or you can take a sculpture class at a local art center or community college and explore varying forms.
- Masks are a most interesting sculptural form. They can be made with a wire base and paper mâché strips (the kind used to make casts for broken bones) and painted. They can also be embellished with hair, feathers, jewels, all kinds of cool stuff.
- Assemblages are a mixed-media art form where found objects are brought together to form an image. Assemblages often include a painted background with the objects attached to it, in a form of collage. Both natural and manmade objects can be used. You could paint a wooden bowl to look like a bird's nest and then put wooden or stone eggs in it, for example.
- The sculptural forms above are both "building-up" sculptures where you shape and add to the form. There are also "taking-away" sculptures where you carve away material to create the shape or face or object. Wood-carving, stone-carving, and some forms of clay work fall into this category.

A word about taking on big projects.

Nothing makes me feel more connected to my artmaking than having a big project going on. Each morning when I sit down to the computer or each time I go to the studio, I know exactly what to work on. When I'm not working on the project, I think about it. At odd moments (in the shower, on the treadmill, driving to an appointment), I'll get insights or ideas or solutions to problems on the project. That deep sense of ongoing involvement in my creative life is a source of great meaningfulness and satisfaction to me.

While you may want to play small in your creative self-expression at first, consider taking on a big project. Remember it isn't the product that's important, it's the process, and a big process is sometimes way more fun than a little one.

Some ideas for big projects

- Write a series of poems on a topic rather than just one. Determine the number of poems in advance. When you've written all the poems, see how they fit together into a whole. Consider creating a chapbook of them (a self-published collection) to give to friends and family.
- Write a novel from a prompt. All three of the novels I've written started out as 10-minute prompts about fictional characters. Each time I knew it was an intriguing start to something. I wanted to know what happened to these people. How they got to this moment and what happened after. Don't know anything about writing a novel? Who cares? You can always learn. The apprenticeship continues.
- Hone your dialog skills by writing a play. Write a trilogy of them.
- Push your song-writing into an opera or a musical play.
- Make a series of quilts depicting some important aspect of your world or the larger one. Or make a huge quilt made up of many scenes.
- Knit individualized Christmas stockings for each member of your extended family.

CREATIVITY AND 12 STEPS: PERSEVERANCE

Continuing to take a personal inventory

It's so easy to give up. And it can be so hard to keep trying, especially in the face of failure. I started working with encaustic paint (colored pigment that is suspended in melted beeswax and resin) in 2006. In the years since, I've taken a bunch of classes, joined the local chapter of the International Encaustic Artists, gone to conferences, and made a lot of really bad paintings (or at least a lot that I didn't find very visually pleasing).

And yet, even though I made a lot of "bad" paintings, I've kept at it. Why? Because I enjoy the process, I'm challenged by the medium, and I can see the potential in it. With encaustic, I can do all the layering and combining I ever wanted to do. So, I've kept at it, and I've gotten better. More important, I keep checking in, taking creative inventory and seeing where else I can challenge myself.

The essence of perseverance is "one day at a time." We focus on the next step, and the next step only. We work on what's in front of us, and we develop a regular practice. Everyone's regular practice will look different; some days I'm still struggling to find mine. I tend to work in fits and starts, but always with something on my calendar (a class, a retreat, a studio day, a friend's upcoming birthday) that gets me back in the studio, working with the wax and the color and the images.

Perseverance, or *grit*, it turns out, may be more important for our success than intelligence or talent. It helps to establish a practice, a way of making art regularly—one small step at a time—to support our attitude of perseverance. I haven't found a regular practice that I maintain, but I continue to try new things! And in that, perhaps I've found a practice.

—Bridget

Question: What might your regular creative practice look like? Will you commit to making 52 collages a year, writing for an hour every morning, or something else?

Suggestion: Start small. Commit to something doable and then once you've been successful, continue to challenge yourself.

SPIRITUAL AWARENESS

CONNECTING WITH THE HIGHER POWER

The origins of the 12-Step program lie in a firm faith in a Higher Power and in the related power of prayer and meditation. For some of us, these ideas are difficult to grasp when we get into recovery. We have worked hard to not depend on anybody, especially something or someone unseen and unknowable. Fortunately, the program is open to all beliefs and non-beliefs, all interpretations of the Higher Power. It is a spiritual program of suggestions, not a religious program of rules and doctrines.

Bit by bit, sometimes quickly, sometimes slowly, most of us come to some form of a comfortable and comforting understanding of a spiritual component to recovery that works for us. We repeat the Serenity Prayer at meetings or listen respectfully. We work through Steps 6 and 7 and release our defenses, our cynicism and resignation, as recovery gives us a chance at a different life.

Creative self-expression is a perfect way to explore and deepen the spiritual aspects of our recovery. Most early art may well have been in service to people's beliefs in gods and spirits. Early cave paintings, early sculptures, early songs have all been attributed to prayers for safety and plentiful food or acts of gratitude for the same.

Artmaking can be viewed as a sacred container, as a way to explore our connection with the Higher Power, a way to open a consideration of the spiritual into our lives.

An Art-Builder's Story

For me, artmaking was primarily finding my passion and following where it led me. I started working with my hands (and mind) at a very early age but I got derailed when I was introduced to mood-altering chemicals. One of the most devastating effects of chemical abuse is that the priority becomes buying, stealing, selling, using, and recovering from the effects of the chemical...day after day.

I have been fascinated with all things that exist in the third dimension— birds, planes, kites, clouds, stars—ever since I can remember. Designing and building RC [radio-controlled] planes enriches my life in every way. I've been making and building stuff since I was a kid. In sobriety, I have a much better record of finishing what I start.

I believe creative self-expression is a gift that is given to anyone who is able to subdue their ego. I believe this is the main track of both sobriety and artistic creativity. I think that building and creating is something that will automatically occur to anyone who pursues a path of listening, trusting, and following an inner voice. In the program tradition, the voice is referred to as a Higher Power, but I believe it is the same force in all traditions: God, Buddha, Jesus, Mohammed. Same force, different names. I think of myself more as a counterfeiter than an artist. I think the best humankind is capable of is counterfeiting...God creates, the rest of us just re-arrange.

—Joe C., freelance iconoclast, Naples, Florida/St. Paul, Minnesota

Some ways to connect your artmaking and spiritual awareness

- Consider creating a series of paintings or drawings, either abstract or representational, that explore your understanding of Spirit.
- Instead of saying your prayers silently, write them in a journal.
- Write your prayers as poems.
- Write a series of poems that express your gratitude for all the blessings of your life.
- Write a series of letters to your Higher Power or other inspirational being. My friend Nisi, a Buddhist, believes all her experiences and all the people in her life are her teachers, and she writes creative letters to them that start out "Dear Teacher."
- Create an altar space in your home for objects, photos, and texts that connect you with the Divine. Refresh your altar with new materials every so often, perhaps with each change in the season or on the first of each month.
- Dance your prayers with the music of Gabrielle Roth or other spiritual musicians. I like to chant along with Deva Premal and Miten as I paint. I don't know what the words mean, but I learn the syllables and can feel the emotional connection.
- Sing your prayers or your poems. Make up your own melodies. Create your own hymns to nature or Spirit.
- Create art objects that express your connection to your Higher Power (sculptures, weavings, paintings, poems) and give them away.
- SoulCollage is a process originated by Serena Frost for accessing intuition. It involves creating a deck of cards with deep personal meaning. Soul collage workshops occur with trained facilitators and they are a great way to get started. There is also a soul collage book done by Serena that can guide you. All that is really needed, however, is a pile of images and photos that inspire you, scissors, a glue stick, and a stack of blank cards. You can buy a large sheet of card stock at an art store and get someone to cut it up into the size cards you want. I like working with 4"x6" cards but some people prefer 6"x9" as the images can be more elaborate on a larger card.

CREATING YOUR OWN MEDITATION BOOK

Since Karen Casey first published *Each Day a New Beginning* in 1982, daily meditation books have been a much loved support for those of us in recovery. Many people read a daily meditation as part of their Step 11 work. While there are many excellent books to choose from, making your own can be a rich and wonderful creative and spiritual experience.

Getting started with your own meditation book

- Begin to gather images that are meaningful to you. Use art books at Goodwill or thrift stores (yes, it's okay to cut them up). Travel magazines, family photos, greeting cards, catalogs, websites are all good sources of images. Cut or tear them out. Large clear plastic file folders or sleeves are good ways to store them. You can sort and create a category system that follows your own inclinations. If you're so inclined, use images that you have colored or drawn or painted. You can take photos of them, upload to your computer, and print them out in the size you want.
- Begin to gather quotes, poems, and other pieces of text that are meaningful for you.
- Begin to write your own prayers, poems, and meditations (4-5 sentences in a paragraph are a good length for meditational readings.)
- You may want the text to be uniform: same font, same size type. Take a look at all the fonts that are available to you on your computer and choose something that appeals to you and then print out the texts. You may also want to use colored inks for your text.
- Choose a journal or other notebook with a cover, binding, and paper that please you. Check stationers, art stores, bookstores, or museum stores for one you really like. Lots of blank books are available on line, but it is nice to be able to handle the book before you buy it to be sure it's right for you.
- Some people start with choosing the book, counting the number of pages, and designing the contents from there.
- You may want to create your own blank book for this project. Community colleges and solo artists, among others, offer book-binding classes. Sometimes they supply the papers and cover materials; sometimes you bring your own. Pages are carefully cut to fit the cover, internal covers get decorated, and you stitch the whole thing together. It's a lot fun to do a book-making class.

- A third idea is to alter an existing book. You may have a worn copy of a meditation book of the size you'd like to work with or perhaps you have or can get a duplicate copy. You can paste your images and your text onto those existing pages. You can further enhance the pages with paint, glitter, fabric, stitching, anything you want. Workshops in altering books are increasingly available and there's lots of info online.

CALLIGRAPHY

Calligraphy is the very old art of writing in special scripts (fonts) in pen and ink. Most of us learned two forms of writing in school, printing and cursive (where the letters flow together). But as you know from computer work, there are many fonts available and calligraphers learn to do one or more specialty fonts by hand. It takes a lot of practice but is very meditative both in the learning and doing.

One of calligraphy's early uses was in the creation of beautiful sacred texts (before the invention of the printing press) and calligraphy continues to have many sacred uses. Calligraphers are often asked to copy a special poem or spiritual saying that gets framed and hung in the home.

Getting started with calligraphy

- Beginning classes are available in many places: community colleges, art schools, and through master calligraphers.
- Books and kits are also available and calligraphy is something you can teach yourself to do.
- Art stores carry many appropriate pen nibs (the correct shapes for making the letters) and inks. Online stores carry specialty inks in metallic colors and special thicknesses.
- There is a wealth of paper to choose from, including luscious handmade papers.
- Calligraphy can also be used to embellish collages, paintings, altered books, anything you can imagine.

CREATIVITY AND THE 12 STEPS: SPIRITUAL AWARENESS

Seeking through prayer and meditation

Artmaking is my primary spiritual practice. When I say this, I mean that it's the primary way that I stay connected to Spirit. There are other ways that I experience Spirit—movement, being in Nature, friends—but creative self-expression is the primary one. In artmaking, I am reminded of why I'm here. I lose myself, and I move to the awareness that I am only a small piece of something much greater.

I have a ritual before heading into the studio. I make coffee or tea; I put on my apron. I turn on the lights and then the griddles that melt the wax. I look over the previous day's work; I tidy and sort. In addition, from almost every place in my garage studio, I can see my altar. On the altar, I keep gifts from students, a candle, a shell, a stone. I also fill and surround the altar with images of the archetypal aspects of the Divine that are most compelling to me: Quanyin and the Virgin of Guadalupe, bearers of unconditional compassion; Ganesh, remover of obstacles; Sarisvati, the teacher; Kali, the protector/destroyer; and images of the Buddha, who represents mindfulness for me. Similarly, I'm fascinated by art that is created as part of spiritual celebrations and rituals (like ceremonial masks and offerings), as well as artwork that is created to teach about or support a spiritual tradition (like Christian icons and Buddhist mandalas).

All of these create a space, a ritual, and a sacred attitude that help remind me of my connection to something greater than myself.

—Bridget

Question: Is there art that you can make to support your own spiritual journey, or an element of ritual that you can develop in your artmaking practice?

Suggestion: Consider developing your own meaningful tradition or ritual for starting your creative time.

SERVICE

SHARING WHAT YOU MAKE AND WHAT YOU KNOW

Service to others is a major part of the recovery path for many of us. We serve as treasurer for our group or greet newcomers. We sponsor others. We clean up the wreckage of our past. We start paying attention not only to our own well-being but to the well-being of others, whether that be physical, emotional, or spiritual.

Several forms of artmaking can be considered service arts as they directly serve others. Preparing a well-cooked and delicious meal is an art when it is done with care and attention to the details, whether you are cooking for yourself or for others. Teaching others what you know about artmaking is another wonderful way to share what you have. Or you can host low-key gatherings to encourage the creativity in others.

Even a solitary act of creating in itself is a gift to the world. There is a different energy that comes from inventing, from creating, from making. It's an energy of vitality, of aliveness, and for many of us, an energy of satisfaction and joy. Contributing that energy by making art in any form is a gift to us all.

ARTFUL COOKING

Many of us fed ourselves poorly, if at all, in our active addictions. We may have fed our families poorly too, just hoping to get them full rather than nourished. Creating beautiful food for ourselves and others is a healing, creative experience.

One of the most artful things about cooking can be its presentation. Simple corn muffins can be brought to the table in a basket lined with a red cloth napkin. Instead of chopping eggplant, tomatoes, cheese, my friend Susan slices them and layers them into a colorful stack held together with a sprig of rosemary. There are always ways to make things beautiful.

And beauty is an essential part of artmaking. Beauty comes in many forms, both dark and tragic/light and joyful. It has room for our suffering and pain; it can soothe our fragile nerves; it can express our deep gratitude. It aligns with many tastes. Everyone is touched by beauty.

Getting started with artful cooking

- Use the best, freshest ingredients that you can afford.
- Give yourself plenty of time in the kitchen. Move slowly and thoughtfully. Make it a spiritual practice.
- Like most art forms, cooking is part art, part science. Learn the things you need to know about techniques and measurements. Just as we learn which brush is best for water color, so we can learn chopping techniques or how to knead bread dough. Lots of classes are available in cooking skills and there's a wealth of information on the Internet as well.
- Many good cooks start out following the recipe, then fine-tune the recipe, then make their own recipes. This art form is no different from the other art media where we learn the basics and then create our own styles.
- You may also be an experimenter, willing to try odd combinations of foods to see what happens. There are endless possibilities.

TEACHING WHAT YOU KNOW TO OTHERS

The 12-Step programs rely heavily on informal teaching. Sharing our experience, strength, and hope in meetings is a long-standing tradition of teaching by story. When we follow the guidance that appears in the Big Book, we are exposed to the teachings of the founders, in particular Bill W., who wrote much of the text. And when we work with sponsors, they teach us what has worked for them.

In my part of the country, many creative teaching and learning opportunities are opening up.

- Artmaking in its many forms is taught in community college classes, both for credit and through non-credit community options.
- Art schools offer classes to the public.
- Professional artists take on apprentices and offer workshops.
- A wealth of information, both written and videoed, exists online.

Getting started as a teacher

I did my first creativity teaching in the late 1990s. I got interested in the *chakras*, energy centers in the body that are part of the Hindu belief system. I wanted to read a book about creativity and the chakras, and I couldn't find one. Knowing that I learn from teaching, I offered a small group of three friends an 8-week class and kept one step ahead of them in my learning. I did all the exercises with them and we had a great time. I've gone on to teach that class numerous times.

- As you develop your own art skills, techniques, and ideas, you may want to share them with others. As in the knitting circles mentioned above, inviting a few like-minded creatives to join you for mutual sharing and teaching is a simple and effective way to start. Painting, writing, collaging, cooking, calligraphy, knitting—many of the arts lend themselves to working in the same space, either in silence or in conversation. Getting people together to work on their projects is a gift and an excellent way to do some informal teaching.

- If you think you might like to take teaching further, take a few workshops with teachers who have good reputations. During the workshop, you can both participate and learn new things and watch how they conduct the group. You might even contact them beforehand and volunteer to assist so you can see first hand how to handle the many details that are involved.

- If speaking in front of groups isn't your thing, consider doing some one-on-one coaching or mentoring of another creative. You could meet once or twice a month for an hour over tea and share your creative experience, strength, and hope with them. You might agree to offer small assignments ("make a list of big projects you'd like to tackle and email me the list; then pick one and take a first step towards completing it") and you might agree to do the same assignment for yourself. Just as sponsoring is often more helpful for the sponsor than the sponsee, so is coaching or mentoring another creative.

- If you're interested in pursuing the idea of creativity coaching, look into the online workshops of Dr. Eric Maisel (www.ericmaisel.com). His creativity coaching classes have been wonderfully helpful to me, both in my own creative work and in my coaching of others.

- When you think you're ready to offer your workshop, you may want to start small, with 4-6 participants in your home. That way you don't have a facilities fee to pay and you can charge a modest amount as you work out the kinks. Or you may want to team up with a more experienced workshop leader, and co-present the workshop. My brother-in-law David Cobb now offers international nature photography workshops. He started out assisting a local photographer who had a large client list. After several years, the older photographer retired, and David bought his business list and has now developed his own reputation and following.

- Contact your local community college or parks and recreation district about teaching a class. These are generally not very well paid as the classes are inexpensive; however, such classes are a great way to meet potential participants for your own private workshops or coaching.

HOSTING SPACE FOR THE CREATIVITY OF OTHERS

When I attended my first writing retreat, I fell in love with the whole experience. It was like camp for grown-ups and a deep spiritual experience all in one. We wrote all day in silence together. We could write in our rooms or in the common areas or down in the meeting hall with its view of the meadow and the mountains in the distance. In the late afternoons, we met in circle in the hall. We followed simple rituals, checked in about how we were doing, got some teachings and coaching, and read to each other. It was wonderful, and I could hardly wait to go again.

I did go again and worked with the same teacher. Then I realized that I had learned what I could from her and that I just needed to spend considerable time writing. But I didn't want to write on my own. So I began to satisfy my need for community by hosting space for the writing and creativity of others.

Getting started with hosting

- *Writing Fridays:* On Fridays, when I am in town, I host other writers in my home. A small group of women (4-5) arrive at 10. We hold circle and set intentions for the day, then move out into writing spaces until lunch at 12:30. We hold silence so that we can write, read, dream, reflect, nap, rest, whatever we need. Lunch is brown bag although occasionally someone will bring something to share as well. In the summer, we eat outside; the rest of the year, we sit around my small dining table and eat and talk and laugh. About 1:20, we head back into silence until 3:15 when we gather in closing circle and those who want to read a few pages aloud do so. We close up at 4. I don't charge for Writing Friday, I just host.

- *Weekend mini-retreats:* Once a quarter, I host a free mini-retreat at my house. We start Fridays at 10, have circle at 5 pm, followed by supper. Some participants will bring sleeping bags and stay over; others head home for the night. Saturday we start at 10 again and go until after supper. Sunday we go 9-noon. Again, we maintain silence during the day, except at meals and during circle. The same group comes for the whole weekend and we develop a lovely rapport and closeness.

- *Week-long retreats out of town:* Once I had caught the retreat bug, I wanted to do it again. So I arranged with the retreat center on Whidbey Island to come at an off-season time by myself. I had a couple of friends living on the island and they met in circle with me. Then I began inviting writing friends to come along. Now a small group of us goes over 4th of July and New Year's every year. We each get our own room, share cooking (each person buys and cooks for the group one day of the retreat), and keep silence during the day. In the evening, we play cards and other games, do collage or draw, or just have great conversations about anything and everything. I don't charge a fee for these retreats as I'm not leading them; rather, I host them so I can be in retreat myself.

- The Whidbey retreats were such a success that I began working with others who didn't want to travel so far from Portland. Now in early spring and late fall (again off-season to keep the costs low), we rent a big house (number of bedrooms = number of participants) on the Oregon coast and spend a week following the Whidbey schedule of silence until 5, circle, supper, and games.

- Not everyone who comes on retreat has to be a writer. At the coast retreat, one regular participant is a painter, one works in mosaics, and the rest of us write. But sometimes people will come just for the silence and the community and rest and read and dream. Our creativity needs that silence and that support, even if we produce very little. Process, remember, not product.

A word about routine, regularity, and ritual.

One of the things I value most about writing and creativity retreats are their basis in what Eric Maisel calls the three "R's" of creativity: routine, regularity, and ritual. When I write or paint every day on a retreat, these activities become routine. My mind, spirit, and body expect them, and I have grown to need that form of satisfaction in the same way that I used to "need" a drink. When I do my art regularly, it creates a groove in my Self and in my day that makes me happy. And when I include a small ritual in opening and closing my creative session, I add a touch of the sacred and the spiritual, and I have closer contact with my Higher Power. How we each make a space and activity sacred is as individual as we are.

Some small creative rituals

- Light a candle to begin your creative session and blow it out when you are finished.
- Ring a small bell or chime to begin your session and ring it again when you have finished. When you ring the beginning bell, sit for a few seconds and honor the creative impulse in yourself that has brought you to the session. When you ring the closing bell, sit for a few seconds and honor the perseverance that has kept you creating even through disappointment or frustration.
- Create a small altar in your creative area. Whether it's a studio, a closet, or a corner of your kitchen table, you can use a small part for an altar. Your altar can be as simple as a piece of colored construction paper with a votive candle on it, or you can lay down a small cloth for your candle, your bell, and several inspirational objects. You can also build or keep your altar in a shoe box or other container when you aren't creating.
- You may wish to pick a talisman for a creative project. Maybe there's a photo that represents the writing you are doing or a postcard of a painting by an artist who inspires you. Maybe it's a stone or a rock or a feather. A writer of my acquaintance always drapes a shawl made by her grandmother over her chair when she sits down to write.
- You may wish to listen to sacred music while you paint or sew or make pots. I like Gregorian chants for painting and Japanese flute for writing.
- Some artists meditate before beginning a creative session; some say a prayer of thanks or dedication.

CREATIVITY AND THE 12 STEPS: SERVICE

Carrying the message

The 12 Steps culminate in giving back. Similarly, a lot of artmaking processes may not feel complete until they are shared with an audience—the dance performed, the poem published, the painting shown. For me, the artwork I've donated to charity fundraisers, the classes I've taught, the articles I've written, even the gallery shows and community events I've participated in are not just about getting the work in front of an audience: they are a form of service. I'm sharing my discoveries, my experiences, my hope, my skills, and even my unique vision of the world.

Translating your own creativity into service may include sharing art materials with a local rehab center, starting up a regular artmaking session for your friends, or even working through this book with other friends in recovery.

That said, simply making art, making something beautiful or cathartic, has value in and of itself. Doing something positive and creative in the world has value. This can be hard to remember. Making art, especially work that doesn't bring you money or fame, can feel like a poor use of your time. Yet its value to us—and to the community—is deeper than the usefulness of the final product. When I spend time being creative, I am more grounded, less anxious, less grumpy. And so I am more present for friends and family, I am more generous with my students, and I have more energy for my life.

Making art fills the well that I draw from in my service to others, just as my art often plays a role in the service I provide to the community. Let your own art first fill your own well, and then consider how you can give back.

—Bridget

Question: How might you use your creative practice to regularly "fill your own well?" How might you use it to give back to others?

Suggestion: Giving others permission to be creative is an easy and wonderful gift to give.

Sober Play

WRITING

- Write a love poem to your favorite food or article of clothing or sports team.
- Select a difficult moment from your past. Write about that moment as a scene in a novel or play just as it happened.
- Write a description of someone you see on the bus, at the mall, or at the grocery store. Start with a description of what they look like. Then, write about why they might be there and what they are going to do next.

ARTMAKING

- Work on a second illuminated manuscript. Pick a favorite poem, quote, or inspirational saying. Pick out the key words or letters you want to emphasize. Then copy the quote in pencil onto a piece of blank paper and use collage images or your own drawings and doodles to illustrate, enhance, or emphasize those key words.
- Play favorites. Consider your favorite color. Go through magazines and find cut out everything you can find in that color. Make a collage using only that color.
- Do a blind drawing. Pick a simple object in the room. Put a pencil to paper, and look closely at the object. Without lifting your pencil from the paper or looking down at the paper, begin to draw the object. Pretend your eyes are connected to your hand and that the movement of your eyes across the object controls the movement of the pencil across the paper. Try it several times.

Part IV
My Journey as a Self-Expressed Creative

Creating is its own reward.

—Pamela K. Metz, *The Creative Tao*

1 When creativity came knocking on my door

Artmaking was not a part of my first year of sobriety. I had all I could do to manage twice-daily meetings, work with my sponsor, juggle three part-time jobs (I had been "let go" from my full-time teaching job five months before I got sober), and try to revive a dying relationship with my partner of 10 years.

I had been a stay-at-home drunk and after the treatment center, I spent very little time in my apartment. I'd work all day, come home and go for a run, shower, and go to a meeting. When the meeting was at 8, I'd go to an early movie at the local mall and then go to the meeting. I was terrified to spend much time alone with myself. The physical need for alcohol had left but the desire to drink felt as strong as ever.

Just before my one-year anniversary, I moved north to a new teaching job. It was a good move as the job helped me redeem myself as a sober professional. But I was terribly lonely. I still went to a ton of meetings but in-between I didn't know what to do with myself. I could no longer spend endless hours watching TV; it was too stupid. I was too restless to read.

Then, in a quiet way, creativity came knocking on my door. On that trip to a toy store to buy gifts for my nephews, I rediscovered coloring: coloring books and colored pencils and colored markers.

I didn't think of this as creativity or artmaking. It was just something to do, to keep me busy, to keep my mind off the urge to go to the liquor store and start up again. I colored a lot over the next four years. It soothed something in me and supported my recovery. And my friend and collaborator Bridget reminded me recently that coloring was a way of accessing my available creativity—an expression and assertion of my Self through color and an exploration of tiny details. Indeed, for me, coloring was a simple way of making meaning through selecting and completing a design. I could not have articulated it this way but it makes sense to me now.

2 Finding the *Artist's Way*

In my fifth year of sobriety, I moved again, this time back home to the Pacific Northwest. Once more I felt lost. I had meetings, of course, but the close-knit program community of small-town Western Pennsylvania didn't translate into this new urban area. I had family, but they already had busy lives. And so the restlessness and loneliness returned.

Then, a major event in my creative recovery happened. At a workshop I attended in the San Juan Islands, I found a copy of Julia Cameron's *The Artist's Way* at the bookstore. As the clerk sold it to me, she asked me if I was an artist. Without thinking about it, I said yes although I had never thought of myself that way. Some intuitive part of me was speaking up for me, moving me in a new direction. I know now that that was my available creativity.

3 Coming to know satisfaction

It is not an exaggeration to say that Cameron's book changed my life. And it was no accident. Cameron, a self-avowed recovering alcoholic, had created a 12-week, 12-part program to help people regain a connection to their creative selves. Not focused on artmaking in particular, her book encourages the use of "morning pages" (daily journaling), meditation, and "artist's dates" to get in touch with our creativity.

Her book was an invitation to step further and more fully onto a path that I was already on, although I couldn't have said so then. I did her program on Saturday afternoons after my regular 12-Step group. It was the summer of 1996 and I would go to a local food court with a nice patio and have a sandwich and an iced latte and read the week's chapter and do the exercises. For the first time in sobriety, I felt fully engaged. What's more, for those two hours, I was happy and satisfied.

4 Discovering my passion for color

When I was 11, I dreamed of being a writer. I wrote stories in spiral notebooks and illustrated them with pictures cut out of magazines. (I still have these notebooks.) I expected Cameron's book to open a door into writing for me. Instead, it did something completely unexpected. It uncovered for me my deep love of color, a love that had been trying to get my attention with those coloring books.

On the last of the 12 Saturdays, sitting outside in the cool September sun, sad that the book was over, I thought about what I could do next. I was still planning to be a writer so I got out my notebook and prepared to make a list of thrilling ideas for novels and short stories. But nothing came. Not a single idea. I began to get frustrated. Where was the flow of creativity that Cameron had implied would happen?

So I went about it a different way. I looked back through my notebook and put a star by each exercise or artist's date that had been really fun. The art museum. A fabric store. A bead store. An art gallery. Listing things I would like to try. Doing a collage. Creating an image file. Doodling while listening to music.

None of these were about writing. Most of these were about color. And then just like that, I knew what was next. I wanted to learn to paint.

5 Deciding to learn to draw

I expected a lot of trepidation to come up, a lot of resistance. I had never shown any ability with drawing or painting. I had no obvious talent. But the naysayer voices in my head were silent. Instead, I was okay with knowing nothing, with being the absolute beginner that I was.

No one was more surprised by this than me. Driven by fear and insecurity, in my drinking years I always needed to know what I was doing, or at least to look like I did. That seemed the only way to survive. But working the Steps, particularly Step 1, had taught me that humility and a willingness to learn, what the Buddhists called *beginner's mind,* was the only path to sobriety. Maybe it could also be the path to satisfaction.

I began looking for a teacher or a class. Portland has several art schools, colleges, really, but they were for artists, those select few who made it to eighth grade and were still raising their hands. The community college had classes for hobbyists and I looked at some of those but couldn't find out anything about the teachers. I knew that I needed more encouragement than instruction and I was aware that my available creativity was fragile. So I kept looking.

6 When the student is ready, the teacher will appear

One day, after a movie downtown with my sister, I went into a big toy store looking for more coloring books. They didn't have anything interesting and so I went into an art store down the street. I don't think I had ever been in an art store before. Even when I was doing the artist's dates with the *Artist's Way,* it hadn't occurred to me.

I wandered slowly down the aisles of paint and paintbrushes, colored pencils and markers, papers and instructional books. I liked the feel of the place, and I especially liked looking at all the ways to work with color. I didn't buy anything—they didn't have coloring books—but on my way out, I found a display of flyers announcing contests, calls for submission, and class offerings. That is where I found the flyer for the Drawing Studio, the next stop on my journey.

7 Finding Phil

Phil Sylvester runs the Drawing Studio out of an old appliance store in my part of town. He has his own studio in half the space where he draws, paints, and makes art guitars. The other half of the space, the store front, is a classroom. Several nights a week and on Saturdays he holds beginning and intermediate drawing classes. Phil is mostly self-taught (his education was in math and architecture), and he does not teach volume or perspective or any of the traditional art school techniques. Instead he teaches observation and courage.

Phil believes that every person can draw and they can draw something satisfying and pleasing to them. He preaches this in class, encouraging students to break the rules, follow their instincts, put down on paper what they see. This was exactly what I needed.

I still had no original talent for drawing, but my early efforts were no worse than those of most of the other students who had had no practice at drawing, for that's what it takes: practice: patience, courage, willingness. Just like recovery.

8 Being willing to make crappy art

I took Phil's introductory class three times. We worked with graphite and charcoal and erasers. simple materials that let us focus on what we were seeing, not on the tools. The goofy techniques he had us do, like turning the paper upside down half-way through the drawing, helped keep me playful, and I got some good practice in ignoring the voice of my inner critic. Beginning drawing classes were a good place for me to practice doing the footwork (or handwork) and letting go of the outcome. Then, after dozens of crappy drawings, I suddenly began to turn out things that were not half-bad.

I moved to the intermediate class and bought my first color tools: soft pastels (an artist's form of chalk). Phil doesn't "teach" pastels, but he was fine with me using them in his class. I loved the color work right from the beginning, and I began to make drawings that were better and better. I began to hang my work in my home office on a set of bulletin bars (cork strips for the wall). I got deep satisfaction from making these pieces. I got deep satisfaction from looking at them. Having other people like them was frosting on the cake. It was nice to hear them ooh and aah, but that was not the main thing. It was my own sense of satisfaction that was important.

9 Drawing makes me feel better

For the next 10 years, I continued to work at the Drawing Studio. I had no place to do chalk work at home. There's a fine dust that comes off the drawings, and I didn't want it all over my living space. So I took classes from Phil for a while and just worked in the corner while he taught the others. Then I began just paying him from time to time to show up and paint.

I had half a dozen shows of my work in cafés and coffee shops around town, but the framing fees were steep and I sold only a few pieces. And I didn't have any ambition to be a professional artist. That wasn't why I painted—to make money or be famous. I did it because it made me feel better, because it was a meaningful experience that satisfied part of that deep longing within me. Drawing had begun to help fill the hole in my soul.

10 The happiness of painting regularly

I began looking for studio space where I could paint more regularly. But my limited budget and my infrequent visits to the Drawing Studio, even when my schedule was open, made spending $400 to $500 a month just not feasible. I kept studio space on my wish list for the next five years.

Then last March an email came across my desk. A friend of a friend was looking for someone to take over her studio in an artists' cooperative. When I read the information, I knew it was for me. It was 10 blocks from my house, $219 a month, and 12'x16'—a big, real space for me to paint in.

I moved in May 1. And now I paint 3-4 mornings a week and each time I go, I get a dose of pure happiness and satisfaction.

11 Putting glue to paper

There are several other facets to my creative life. One is collage—putting glue to paper. A few years after I discovered the Drawing Studio, I met a wonderful painter named Linda Sawaya, who offers collage classes in her garage studio in the northwest hills of Portland. I took workshop after workshop from her, finding something immensely soothing in cutting images out of magazines and arranging them in interesting patterns on paper.

I began collecting images from catalogs, greeting cards, magazines, calendars. Our world offers a wealth of images. I keep them in the big boxes that come with my walking shoes. For a while I worked large—on poster board—and very small—on business cards. One day I got the idea to create the collages in a blank journal someone had given me that had pages made from file folders. The heavy backing was perfect and the book was a convenient way to store the images. I've now filled five such books.

12 Stepping into my writing life

And beginning in 2000, I finally started writing. After attending a Buddhist retreat on writing and the Dharma (the Buddhist teachings), I gathered with a small group of women, all beginning writers, and we started writing our spiritual histories, using a wonderful book called *Spiritual Rx* by Frederick and Maryann Brussat. Each month we'd write a three-page story about some life experience with an aspect of spirituality such as silence or meditation or grace or prayer. Then we'd gather and read them to each other in supportive witness.

Two years later, in 2002, I travelled up to Whidbey Island just north of Seattle and took a writing workshop, Self as Source, from author Christina Baldwin, whose book *Life's Companion: Journal Writing for the Spiritual Quest*, had helped me start journaling in sobriety. I met more writers, and I loved the writing retreat idea and could hardly wait to come back.

My writings got deeper and stronger, and I began to commit to myself also as a writer.

13 Developing a creative life

In 2007, I self-published my memoir, *Sober Truths: The Making of an Honest Woman*. That led to some wonderful friendships and a chance to tour the country with Hazelden Treatment Centers speaking to women in recovery. It also confirmed my writing life.

After my memoir was completed, I wrote a lot of prompts (short, timed writings). Then because I was working with clients who were writing novels, I decided to see what writing one was like. My 11-year-old self was finally getting her wish. It took me two years but was really fun. Since then I have written two more books. I do morning pages every morning, and I do some creative writing every morning. I do collage with friends, and I go to the studio. Exercising my available creativity and engaging in creative self-expression are often the most satisfying times of each day. I usually do them early, to guarantee myself a meaningful start to the day.

I don't want to make it sound like creativity is my whole life. It isn't. I have a business (freelance editing and creativity coaching), and I have to market my services and work for my clients 40 and sometimes 50 hours a week. I go to meetings, sponsor other women, work out regularly, have a social life. But creative self-expression has become a regular part of my life, and my life is richer and I am happier for it. I know that my sobriety is stronger for it as well.

Sober Play

WRITING

- Identify a problem of your own you would like to solve. Write a dialog between you and the problem.
- Grab the book nearest you and turn to page 52. Now, pick any three words on the page. Next, write a haiku using those three words. A haiku is a simple, non-rhyming poem that has 5 syllables in the first line, 7 syllables in the second line, and 5 syllables in the third line. The poem doesn't have to make sense. Just try to conjure an interesting image or make a compelling comparison.
- Play Mad Libs™ with a friend. Ask them for a profession or type of person, a plant or animal, a location or setting, an object, two adjectives, and a problem. Then, each write a short story that incorporates all of these.

ARTMAKING

- Blind drawing. Look in the mirror. Put pencil to paper, and without lifting your pencil from the paper or looking at what you're drawing, draw your own face.
- Cutting color #1. Cut random shapes out of colored construction paper. The shapes can be circles, squares, or anything else. They can be all the same, or they can be different. Experiment with arranging the shapes in different ways. When you find an arrangement that pleases you, use a glue stick to glue them to a piece of blank paper.
- Cutting color #2. Cut out a number of circles or squares or triangles in varying sizes from colored construction paper. Make an arrangement with the circles or squares or triangles that you find appealing. Draw patterns on the colored shapes to add variety if you like.

Part V
Finding Your Creative Path

The creative person lets go of expectations
And is surprised at the results.
She lets go of plans, and new works create themselves.

—Pamela K. Metz, *The Creative Tao*

1 Finding your way into creative self-expression

It may be that in reading these pages you know already what form of expression you want to pursue. You may have known as a kid that you wanted to be a writer or a painter. Maybe you've always doodled and would like to be a cartoonist or caricaturist. Maybe you loved playing with clay and mud as a kid and would like to investigate making pottery. Maybe you used to knit or crochet or sew and you'd like to see where playing with fibers and fabrics might take you. Maybe you've been gardening or cooking more since you got sober and those might be great canvases for your creativity. Maybe voice lessons or dance lessons would make your heart sing.

Remember we're not talking talent here. We're talking interest and inclination.

2 Help in finding your medium of expression

Or it may take some time to settle on what art medium speaks to you most. I've tried out lots of things: bookmaking, book altering, visual journaling (it's not really for me), process painting, dancing my story (so not for me!). If you're unclear as to what creative form might please you, that's okay. We all have to start somewhere. You might consider committing six months to exploration.

Here are some suggestions for that exploration:

- Do Julia Cameron's *Artist's Way* by yourself or in a group (check online to find group offerings). As I said earlier, doing this book changed my life. The readings are short; the exercises are fairly simple. I did each chapter in two hours on a Saturday.

- Do Cameron's artist dates. These are weekly experiences for finding your medium and filling your creative well. Here are some of the ones I did: yarn shop, bead store, art gallery, photography gallery, zoo, art museum, history museum, paint your own dish store, a trip to Goodwill for books, an art store, a fabric store. I didn't buy anything except at the bead store (I made an inexpensive necklace), at the paint your dish store (I made a mug), and at Goodwill. The rest of them I just visited and browsed. I was able to eliminate a number of possibilities this way. My favorites: the yarn and fabric stores—all that color and texture!

- Get a creativity buddy and do the first two items above together. Your buddy doesn't need to be in recovery, just interested in creative self-expression.

- Check out what inexpensive classes and workshops are offered by your community/junior college in their public programs. You'll often find an "intro to..." class or workshop in just about anything: watercolor, floral arranging, metal work, calligraphy. Work out your budget and try the ones that seem most intriguing.

3 *Note from Bridget:* The challenge of finding your creative way

Some of us already know what form of creative expression calls to us. Some of us may need no more than five minutes of exploration before we know what we want to do. But for others of us, even six months of exploring and doing all the exercises Jill recommends above still won't be enough. For some of us, finding a medium for creative expression can be a challenge.

We may know that we want to be creative yet feel overwhelmed or intimidated by the options. We may end up trying a number of different things before we find one something—or many things—that feel right. You may end up changing media or doing more than one. Jill went from coloring books to drawing to pastels, and never gave up collage and writing. For me, I love layering and piecing, and I've done that in fiber, writing, performance, collage, costuming, jewelry-making, process painting, sculpture and encaustic.

Or you may feel called to do something—like Jill felt called to be a writer and I felt called to be a painter—but find that your path leads you in other directions for a time. It took me ten years of sobriety before I had the courage and the resilience to begin painting again.

By far, the easiest and simplest creative self-expression starting point is to get yourself a pencil and a blank notebook. Journaling, doodling, sketching, and jotting down ideas are all low-pressure introductions to writing, drawing, and discovering what you love. You can use the blank notebook to do some of the *Sober Play* writing and art explorations in the back of this book. Or for a simple introduction to combining writing and doodling, try the exercises in Quinn McDonald's book *Raw Art Journaling*.

4 *Note from Bridget:* Happiness is key

It may sound simple, but the most important thing to look for is something that makes you happy when you do it. It can be tempting to look at somebody else's finished sculpture or drawing or read someone else's novel and say, "I'd like to do something like that." And it can be tempting to say, "I've always wanted to be a romance novelist or sculptor." But don't make your decision on the products you could make or the identity you could take on. Instead, make your decision based on the joy of the process of making those products.

Remember to give yourself time to explore. As you work through this book, underline or put a star by every activity that seems really interesting or excites or inspires you in some way. If you try something and enjoy it, then put another star by it. Finally, make a list of all of those activities. What do they have in common? Is there something you used to love doing as a kid that feels similar or uses the same skills? Asking these questions may give you some insight into what you most want to pursue.

You don't lose anything by dabbling in a variety of media. You'll inevitably learn tricks and tools that you can use no matter what you finally decide on. And just like recovery, creative self-expression is for the long haul and a great way to practice patience.

5 Getting to know your intuition

Finding your way into a form of creative self-expression that works for you is a great, safe way to practice using your intuition, of listening to the affirmative voice inside you. We all have this inner knowing, and many of us drank or used to shut it up. In recovery, we can cultivate that voice.

As you do your artist dates or take intro classes and workshops or work with materials, watch for these tell-tale signs of joy and meaning:

• You get caught up in the making and time goes by surprisingly fast.

• You make yourself proud just by showing up and trying a few things.

• You have a good time making.

• You feel willing to make mistakes and start over.

• You like at least one small aspect of something you made.

• You are excited and maybe even eager to try it again.

We all have the desire to create; we all have the desire to express ourselves. What's right for you is just waiting to be uncovered.

6 Starting out in a low-key way

One of the wonderful things about creative self-expression is that it doesn't have to be expensive. Sure, you can spend a small fortune on art supplies, rent a big studio space, or travel around the world doing workshops and classes with established artists. You can also spend very little and begin having a great time today, in fact, within the next 5 minutes.

- You can put the book down and do one of the *Sober Play* suggestions right now.

- You can go to Goodwill and other thrift stores and buy very inexpensive supplies, many of them unopened.

- You can ask friends, relatives, and neighbors for supplies that they're never going to use.

- You can use the art supplies of your kids and grandkids.

- When Christmas or your birthday comes around, you can ask for a new cookbook or gardening book or a gift certificate to an art supply store or money towards lessons.

- You can watch for a big sale at Michael's craft stores or get supplies on the back-to-school special. I've gotten some great materials at Office Depot.

7 Sticking with it or principles before personality

Many of us have had the experience of immediate enthusiasm and energy for something new, only to see it dwindle away when the novelty wore off. We buy books and read only the first few pages; we get a gym membership and go for two weeks before we become "too busy" to go. What will be different about poetry or painting or pottery? Maybe nothing. Maybe everything.

- If creating doesn't bring you joy and meaning and satisfaction, you won't stick with it. Why should you? The only thing I can flog myself into doing regularly is going to the gym. I have such a commitment to long-term health that I am willing to go four times a week with my gym buddy even though I don't enjoy it while I'm there. I couldn't possibly do that with creativity too. So it's important to find a medium that both satisfies and challenges you. That may take some time, but it's so worth exploring.

- Start out simple and easy so there's satisfaction right away. It can take time to get good at your medium. If I had tried to paint before I had colored for a while, I might never have stayed with it.

- Keep your expectations for quality low and don't compare your work with the work of professionals. If you're learning to play the trumpet, don't compare yourself with Miles Davis at the top of his game. Compare yourself with other beginners. When I took my first drawing class, I thought my stuff was pretty lousy. But when I looked around, my stuff was as good (or bad) as everybody else's in the class.

- Remember: quantity over quality. The way we get better is to make a lot of stuff!

- Our creative practice is a great place to practice dealing with the challenges life throws our way. Frustrated because your sewing machine ate up the expensive silk for your quilt? Breathe through anger. Unhappy because your spouse didn't like your last painting? Let rejection flow through you and on out. Sad because the deer ate all your tulip bulbs for that special flowerbed you worked so hard to design? Don't take it personally.

Creativity is a safe place to work with our feelings, our expectations, our new way of being in life without anesthetic. We can practice doing the footwork and leaving the outcome to our Higher Power. We can practice keeping it simple. We can practice showing up. Remember, the only real way to fail at artmaking of any kind is to not do it.

A word about "I don't feel like it."

A creative practice takes commitment, just like anything else worth doing. There will be plenty of times when you don't feel like going to your pottery class or meeting your writing buddy at the coffee shop or setting up the sewing machine. Do it anyway. In some ways, it's like going to a 12-Step meeting. The people who stay sober are the ones who keep going, even when they don't feel like it. And they almost always feel better afterwards.

Eric Maisel says, "Let meaning trump mood." Your opportunity to find meaning and satisfaction in creative self-expression can become so reliable that it will pull you out of the blues and into a better space. And if it doesn't, what better thing to put your blues, your mood into, than a benign act of creating something?

LAST WORDS

The art suggestions we've made here are just for starters. One of the most wonderful things about artmaking is the wealth of possibilities. It's a place where we need never be bored. And as someone who has been bored a lot in her life, I find this really important.

The 12 promises in the program promise us a new freedom and a new happiness. Creative self-expression has been a big support for me in finding these. I hope it can be for you too.

Part VI
A Few More Tools

The more you create, the more creativity is available.
—Pamela K. Metz, *The Creative Tao*

10 WAYS TO GET STARTED AS A CREATIVE

1. Speak of yourself as a creative. When asked "What do you do?" be creative. I'm a creative gardener. Collage artist. Painter. Chef. Garden designer. Who cares if it's just your garden? Speak and it will live.

2. Put together a creativity box: scissors, glue sticks, colored pencils, glitter, feathers, pretty papers, pipe cleaners, photo-rich magazines, marbles, Velcro, whatever appeals to you. Maybe get a large toy box or covered plastic storage box that will hold it all. Take a trip to Michael's or another craft store, set a $ limit, and be creative in your purchases. Then use them whenever you are bored or restless.

3. Get an unlined journal, colored pencils, a sharpener. Develop a brief, daily drawing practice.

4. Try *The Writer's Book of Days* (Judy Reeves) and do a 10-15 minute daily writing practice.

5. Commit to the 12-week program of *The Artist's Way*. You can commit to the full program or just commit to one portion: artist's dates, chapter activities, morning pages.

6. Create an altar. Use a small table, a shelf, a shoebox. Use a shawl, a yard of nice fabric, a scarf, a cloth napkin. Add items important to you emotionally, spiritually, creatively. Change it on an important day of the month.

7. Go boldly into your creative life. Commit to the year program of a book like *Art & Soul* (Pam Grout) or the *Creativity Book* (Eric Maisel). It'll change your life.

8. Spend part of a weekend day in creative mode. Decide for a period of time (I recommend 3-4 hours) that everything you do will come out of your sense of creativity. Stack the dishes in the drainer in an interesting pattern. Wipe the kitchen counter mindfully and artistically. You get the idea.

9. Collect photo- and text-rich magazines for collage work as in *Visioning* (Lucia Cappachione). Create a small (5"x6") collage for each Feng Shui area (called a *gua*) in your home and what you would like to have happen in that part of your life: Wealth, Health, Creativity, Fame and Reputation, Romance and Relationship, Travel and Helpful People, Spirituality, Career.

10. Create a small group of like-minded souls who will meet for a couple of hours once a month and do show-and-tell with creative projects. No judgments, no critiques, just holding a space for each other to risk and share your creativity.

100 PROMPTS FOR WRITING OR OTHER USE

1. Road trip
2. Ice cream
3. Repetition
4. A key
5. Joni Mitchell
6. Accepting an invitation
7. Scars
8. In the scrapbook
9. It doesn't work anymore
10. A house nobody lives in
11. Sitting in a car across the way
12. Changing your name
13. The hand that feeds you
14. The wall of not good enough
15. The long way around
16. The weight of sleep
17. The light was impossible
18. A crossroads
19. A stranger
20. The convenience store
21. What was forbidden
22. An expectation of pleasure
23. Mr. Bear
24. In the mirror
25. A map of his body
26. Drinking ice water in front of the heater
27. What she asked for
28. The last bicycle
29. Burning her hand
30. Grade school karma
31. Communion
32. Reunion
33. It was premature
34. The painting
35. Tired to the bone
36. Anonymous sex, unanimous sex
37. Sleight of hand
38. Out of sight, out of mind
39. If only
40. What if I had…
41. Bliss
42. Out the office window
43. Finding out the truth
44. Getting out the stain
45. Making the bed
46. In the airport
47. Better late than never
48. Doing without tea
49. The elephant under the bed
50. Scissors
51. Tuxedo cat
52. Gold mug
53. The checkbook
54. Sounds in the night
55. Clear sailing
56. The wind came up fast
57. The last of her friends to say something
58. They didn't speak again
59. A yellow highlighter
60. On the bus headed downtown
61. She passed him at the corner
62. The right way
63. The right of way
64. A really bad idea
65. My pajamas
66. A separation from the beginning
67. Too many doors, not enough windows

68.   We suffer well together
69.   Falling on her like a stone
70.   A dance partner
71.   Young and empty
72.   A hard thought
73.   All the old voices
74.   A dress that moved
75.   When I broke the crystal on my watch
76.   Too slow by half
77.   In the studio in the dark
78.   Red leather
79.   What I thought at that moment
80.   Cheerful beyond measure
81.   Vision and revision
82.   In a little town bar
83.   The last aisle I walked down
84.   Last seen
85.   Moonrise over the coast of Maine
86.   Holding it together
87.   A toucan hanging from the ceiling
88.   Red carnations, oeillets rouges
89.   Van Gogh in the afternoon
90.   Nicotine and diet soda
91.   Overwhelmed by solitude
92.   The oldest boy
93.   Down the concrete corridor
94.   Dancing to the kitchen
95.   Restless deep in the bones
96.   Wood and windows
97.   Like the fools we were
98.   Curly and stinky
99.   Purple tulips
100. Her father's disappointment

JILL'S CREATIVE PRACTICE LISTS

I'm a list maker. I found them to be a great organizational tool for me in general, and I have found them invaluable in my creative practice. Making lists helps me dream, plan, and stay on task—all most helpful in fitting creativity into my life. I use several kinds of lists. Perhaps one or more of these will be helpful to you.

My annual creative dream list

Early each year, I make a list of creative goals I'd like to achieve in the coming year. Since this is a wish list, I play really big, putting more things on the list than I can possibly do and including some very risky or outrageous items (like doing a painting workshop in the south of France).

I put down things I'd like to complete, things I'd like to learn or a class I want to take, things I want to practice and get better at, ways I want to get my work out into the world. I refer to the list every few weeks. I cross things off either when I've done them or if I've lost interest in doing them.

I'm a great believer in telling the universe what we want and need, and my dream list is one way of speaking that. I usually write my list with a small group of creative friends at a New Year's gathering, and we read them out loud to each other and discuss them and encourage each other to get even bolder. I had *a studio of my own for painting* on my list for five years. Last year that dream came true.

Although the list serves as a guide and reminder, often my work will take off in a different direction. I don't let that be a problem. I just keep moving in whatever direction seems best.

My creative accomplishments list

Also around New Year's, I make a list of things I've accomplished in the creative realm the year before. Some of them will have been on the dreams list, but others will have been opportunities I've made or taken. This year *worked regularly in my studio* is on the list!

My list includes any classes I took or workshops I attended, any related books I read, any play dates with other creatives I had. It may include a risk I took with new materials or an improvement to my creative space. I give myself lots and lots of credit. When I was drinking, my only goal was to survive another day. Now I have much grander goals. And as one of my teachers Dave Ellis says, "Celebrate everything." It's a great idea to celebrate your accomplishments with other creatives or close friends.

My little creative list

This may be the most important list of all for me. *My little list*, as I call it, is a running to-do list of small tasks and ideas for my creative practice. Most of them can be completed in under an hour, some in under 10 minutes.

When I was first creating, I'd spend a lot of time each session figuring out what to do next. I wanted to use the time in the best possible way. And that indecision created a lot of anxiety. But I don't come to creativity for more anxiety—just the opposite. I want creative sessions to soothe me. So I created the Little List.

At the end of each creative session, I note what to do next on a particular painting or piece of writing. If I'm starting something new, there are always ideas on the Little List. Having a list of small tasks is an effective form of guidance for me. Like many people, I have to fit my creative life into my regular life: job, family, friends, exercise, home and car maintenance. So I don't want to spend a lot of time deciding what to do next. I use the Little List to keep myself focused and to have a variety of things to do and try.

Note from Bridget: If you're not a list-maker, just arrange your creative times so that you leave yourself with a clear next step. If you finish a collage, leave yourself a stack of images you didn't use but found interesting. If you finish a chapter, make a note of three things that you didn't include or are considering. Stopping in the middle of a challenge can be a great way to let your mind work on it until you can get back to the project.

SOBER PLAY

Writing suggestions to get you started

1. Spend a few minutes with a family photo album and choose a photo of a person whose face intrigues you. It may be of a relative you don't know well or at all, it may be of an old friend, it may be of someone loved and lost. Write a letter from that person to you and a letter back from you (make up any details you need). **To take this deeper:** Write a conversation (in dialog form) between you and this person.

2. Open a drawer in your bathroom and take out any three objects. Write a conversation between the objects in which they discuss you. **To take this deeper:** Experiment with turning this conversation into a poem.

3. "When Sally opened the door, a very tiny man stood there holding a very large duck." Write a one-page story that starts with this sentence. **To take this deeper:** Expand the story and see where it leads you.

4. Pick one of these words—*from, that, can, might*—and write an 8-line poem where the end of each line rhymes with that word. **To take this deeper:** Write a poem each with the other three words suggested.

5. Pick a novel off your shelf and open to a page that has dialog. Pick any line of dialog and write a page of the beginning of a story that uses that line somehow. **To take this deeper:** Complete the story.

6. Write 2 different paragraphs that start with same first five words. They can be variations on one idea or completely different from each other. **To take this deeper:** Write 10 sentences that each use all five words.

7. Write a love poem to your favorite food or article of clothing or sports team. **To take this deeper:** Write a whole series of love poems to favorites.

8. Select a difficult moment from your past. Write about that moment as a scene in a novel or play just as it happened. **To take it deeper:** Rewrite the scene with a different ending.

9. Write a description of someone you see on the bus, at the mall, or at the grocery store. Start with a description of what they look like. Then, write why they might be there and what they are going to do next. **To take it deeper:** Work this writing into a short story. Is there a conflict that is started, moved forward, or solved by their visit to the store? What's the resolution?

10. Identify a problem of your own you would like to solve. Write a dialog between you and the problem. **To take it deeper:** Ask a friend to read your part of the dialog and you read the part of the problem.

11. Grab the book nearest you and turn to page 52. Now, pick any three words on the page. Next, write a haiku using those three words. A haiku is a simple, non-rhyming poem that has 5 syllables in the first line, 7 syllables in the second line, and 5 syllables in the third line. The poem doesn't have to make sense. Just try to conjure an interesting image or make a compelling comparison. **To take it deeper:** Write a longer, free-form poem using the same three words or including lines from the haiku.

12. Play Mad Libs™ with a friend. Ask them for a profession or type of person, a plant or animal, a location or setting, an object, two adjectives, and a problem. Then, each write a short story that incorporates all of these. **To take it deeper:** Do a second round but this time, each of you writes half a story and then you each finishes the other person's story.

SOBER PLAY

Artmaking suggestions to get you started

All you need:

- Blank paper, like a stack of copy paper or a sketchbook
- Collage materials (old magazines, junk mail, greeting cards)
- Colored construction paper
- Good sharp scissors
- A glue stick
- Crayons, markers, or colored pencils—some way to add color
- Cheap watercolors or tempera paints
- A cheap paintbrush
- A regular pencil or pen

- **Make something ugly!** Challenge yourself to make something really UGLY! Choose only the ugliest colors of crayons and draw only the ugliest things. Glue down cut out shapes or collage images that will make it even more hideous. Then ask yourself, "What would make this even uglier?" Do it! Have fun with it!
- **Make a collage self-portrait** by piecing together images that represent different parts of who you were, who you are and who you want to be. It doesn't have to look like a person: it's just a collection of images that represent who you are.
- **Make an ink blot critter.** Using watercolors or thin tempera paints, dribble several colors of paint on a piece of paper. Before the paint dries, fold the paper in quarters. Then open it up and let it dry flat. Once it's dry, find crazy animals or creatures in the paint, just like you would find characters in the clouds. Use a pen, pencil, or even crayons to outline the animals, flesh out the shapes (real or imaginary), and add details like eyes, fangs, or whiskers.
- **Do a hand dance.** Listen to music and move a pencil across a paper in response to the music. Don't look at the doodle; just move the pencil for 30 seconds. When the time is up, move to a new sheet of paper. When the music is over, look at your doodles. Pick your favorite and add to the doodle with watercolors or colored pencils. Try filling in the spaces with patterns.

- **Connect the dots.** Draw 50 dots on a page. Now, begin connecting those dots with straight lines. Use any order, just make sure all the dots are connected to at least one other dot. Use the doodle as a basis for coloring or creating patterns.
- **Work on an illuminated manuscript.** Turn to a random page in a book, and pick your five favorite words from the page. Then find collage images or draw pictures that somehow illuminate or illustrate the word. They can do on separate paper or combine to make something interesting. Include the five words in some way if you like.
- **Work on a second illuminated manuscript.** Pick a favorite poem, quote, or inspirational saying. Pick out the key words or letters you want to emphasize. Then copy the quote in pencil onto a piece of blank paper and use collage images or your own drawings and doodles to illustrate, enhance, or emphasize those key words.
- **Play favorites.** Consider your favorite color. Go through magazines and find cut out everything you can find in that color. Make a collage using only that color.
- **Blind drawing.** Pick a simple object in the room. Put a pencil to paper, and look closely at the object. Without lifting your pencil from the paper or looking down at the paper, begin to draw the object. Pretend your eyes are connected to your hand and that the movement of your eyes across the object controls the movement of the pencil across the paper. Try it several times.
- **Blind drawing.** Look in the mirror. Put pencil to paper, and without lifting your pencil from the paper or looking at what you're drawing, draw your own face.
- **Cutting color #1.** Cut random shapes out of colored construction paper. The shapes can be circles, squares, or anything else. They can be all the same, or they can be different. Experiment with arranging the shapes in different ways. When you find an arrangement that pleases you, use a glue stick to glue them to a piece of blank paper.
- **Cutting color #2.** Cut out a number of circles or squares or triangles in varying sizes from colored construction paper. Make an arrangement with the circles or squares or triangles that you find appealing. Draw patterns on the colored shapes to add variety if you like.

RESOURCES

The following list contains sources that have been helpful to us or recommended by others. It also recaps some of the resources mentioned in the text.

Reclaiming Your Creativity
Creative Conversations: ArtMaking as Playful Prayer by Bridget Benton
The Artist's Way and *Walking in This World* by Julia Cameron
The Artist Within: A Guide to Becoming Creatively Fit by Whitney Ferré
Art and Soul by Pam Grout
Pencil Drawing: New Ways to Free Your Creative Spirit by Mari Messer

Upping Your Creativity
Art & Fear: Observations on the Perils (and Rewards) of Artmaking by David Bayles and Ted Orland
Coaching the Artist Within by Eric Maisel
The Creativity Book by Eric Maisel

Coloring Books
www.doverpublications.com
www.amazon.com
Upscale toy stores
Larger art supply stores and online shops

Drawing
Zen Seeing, Zen Drawing: Meditation in Action by Frederick Franck
Zentangle Untangled: Inspiration and Prompts for Meditative Drawing by Kass Hall

Collage
SoulCollage™: An Intuitive Collage Process for Individuals and Groups by Serena B. Frost

Visual Journaling
Raw Art Journaling: Making Meaning, Making Art by Quinn McDonald

Fiber Arts & Mixed Media Arts
Cloth, Paper, Scissors (6 magazine issues a year)

Metal-Smithing
Jewelry Lab: 52 Experiments, Investigations, and Explorations in Metal by Melissa Manley

Poetry
Finding What You Didn't Lose and *Poetic Medicine* by John Fox
In the Palm of Your Hand: The Poet's Portable Workshop by Steve Kowit

Writing
A Writer's Book of Days by Judy Reeves
Life's Companion: Journaling for the Spiritual Quest by Christina Baldwin
The Right to Write by Julia Cameron

ACKNOWLEDGEMENTS

This book was born out of the collective wisdom expressed in thousands of meetings and many dozens of conversations with friends in recovery and friends in creativity. My thinking about creativity has also been strongly influenced by the work of Dr. Eric Maisel, particularly his creativity coaching classes and his book *Natural Psychology*.

Thanks to the creative folks who contributed their stories to the book, and to Karen Casey, Lindy Fox, Beth Easter, and Judith Turian, who offered encouragement and suggestions on an early version of the book.

Huge gratitude to Bridget Benton, whose brilliant contributions have so enriched this book.

And a very special thanks to my sister Kerry, who was the first person to encourage me to get sober and who has championed my creative efforts from the start.

THE AUTHORS

Jill Kelly, PhD, was an intellectual and a cynic until she got into recovery in 1989. Now her mission is to be as creative as possible and to encourage the creativity of others. A former college professor, she makes her living as a freelance editor and creativity coach. She is the author of a memoir, *Sober Truths: The Making of an Honest Woman*, a finalist for the Oregon Book Award, and a novel, *The Color of Longing*. She writes and paints in Portland, Oregon, where she lives with her three cats. Web: www.jillkellyauthor.com. Blogs: www.thewritingwheel.blogspot.com and www.sobertruths.blogspot.com

Bridget Benton, MS, loves making stuff and loves helping other people make stuff. She has been an artist most of her life. She believes that each person has a unique creative voice and supports them in speaking their visual truth. Author of the award-winning book *The Creative Conversation: ArtMaking as Playful Prayer*, she holds an undergraduate degree in art and a Master of Science in Creative Studies. Bridget leads workshops in intuitive creative process in Portland, Oregon, and across the country. Web: www.eyesaflame.com. Email: sparky@eyesaflame.com

Made in the USA
San Bernardino, CA
03 January 2016